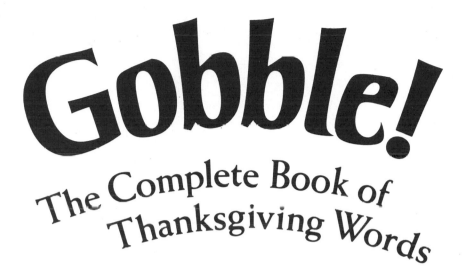

Gobble!

The Complete Book of Thanksgiving Words

BY LYNDA GRAHAM-BARBER

Pictures by Betsy Lewin

BRADBURY PRESS · NEW YORK

Collier Macmillan Canada · Toronto

Maxwell Macmillan International
New York · Oxford · Singapore · Sydney

I would like to thank Carolyn Travers of Plimoth Plantation, and Dr.
Richard L. Stanger, minister, Plymouth Church of the Pilgrims, Brooklyn,
New York, for sharing their bountiful knowledge of the Pilgrims with me.
—L.G.-B.

Bradbury Press
Macmillan Publishing Company
866 Third Avenue
New York, NY 10022

Maxwell Macmillan Canada, Inc.
1200 Eglinton Avenue East
Suite 200
Don Mills, Ontario M3C 3N1

Macmillan Publishing Company is part of the
Maxwell Communication Group of Companies.

First edition
Printed and bound in the United States of America
10 9 8 7 6 5 4 3 2 1
Typography by Cathy Bobak

LIBRARY OF CONGRESS CATALOGING-IN-PUBLICATION DATA
Graham-Barber, Lynda.
Gobble : the complete book of Thanksgiving words / by Lynda
Graham-Barber ; pictures by Betsy Lewin. — 1st ed.
p.   cm.
Includes bibliographical references and index.
Summary: Defines or explains various words commonly associated
with Thanksgiving, such as "harvest," "Pilgrim," and "musket," and
gives their origin or historical background.
ISBN 0-02-708332-2
1. Thanksgiving Day—Juvenile literature. [1. Thanksgiving Day.
2. English language—Etymology.] I. Lewin, Betsy, ill. II. Title.
GT4975.G73   1991
394.2'683—dc20   90-22770

A thankful heart is not the greatest virtue,
but the parent of all the other virtues.

—CICERO

For all people who journey
in search of freedom

Contents

Hear Ye! Hear Ye!
We celebrate THANKSGIVING DAY,
giving THANKS
on the fourth THURSDAY in NOVEMBER.
Celebrating the HARVEST
is a FALL TRADITION.

Thanksgiving Day

Thanksgiving morning, Anywhere, U.S.A. Instead of the usual jarring "get up now!" call, you sleep late, vaguely aware of soft, muffled sounds of activity and warm smells wafting from the kitchen. You dress just in time to catch the parade, with its high-stepping marching bands and waving dignitaries. Everyone is in an expectant mood, and you are famished after missing breakfast. Finally, after much shuffling of chairs, it's time to eat.

Turkey and stuffing drenched in gravy, squash, cranberry sauce, and three different desserts . . . Soon you feel more stuffed than the plumpest dressed turkey.

Unfortunately, you get the smaller end of the wishbone, which means clean-up detail. Somehow, today, you don't mind. It's Thanksgiving. Besides, your favorite uncle slips you—on the sly—another piece of his famous praline pumpkin pie, while everyone else is fussing over coffee and the television reception for the football game.

Perhaps more than any other national holiday, Thanksgiving captures the essence of America and the unified spirit of all Americans. The fourth Thursday in November, the day on which we give thanks, is an annual observance that crosses all religious boundaries. Not only do we celebrate the courage and conviction of that tiny band of Pilgrims who braved an unknown land in search of religious liberty, but we stop to remember people everywhere still struggling for freedom. And by inviting family and friends to share a bountiful meal, we express gratitude for our own personal gifts and good fortune.

Good fortune was in short supply for the Pilgrims in Plymouth, Massachusetts, during the fall of 1621. Yet despite their hardships, the settlers paused to give thanks for their harvest. But do we give thanks every November because of this Pilgrim harvest holiday? And did the colonists' dinner include modern Thanksgiving staples like turkey, cranberry sauce, and pumpkin pie?

The Pilgrim adventure, from the *Mayflower* voyage to their settlement in Plymouth, has sparked the interest and imagination of people for centuries. For the Thanksgiving story, let's go back to Plymouth Colony in the fall of 1621, and that first fall celebration.

Thanks

We have the Old English word *panc* to thank for giving us our word *thanks*. In its earliest form *panc* means "thought," as in the Bible's (Matthew 15:19) "For out of the heart proceed evil *pances* [thoughts]."

The meaning of *thank* developed from "thought" to "kind thoughts or feeling good will" and, finally, to "being grateful." After all, when you feel kindly toward something or someone, don't you usually feel gratitude, too?

Most of us assume that expressing gratitude and the giving of thanks formed the basis of that first Pilgrim celebration in 1621. Yet there is no documented evidence to back up this assumption.

Suffering from a poor diet and the effects of their first bitter New England winter, over half of the *Mayflower* passengers had died from pneumonia or scurvy that first year. All the crops they'd planted in the spring had failed, except the corn. Weary from burying their dead, the surviving Pilgrims nonetheless decided to set aside a three-day period to celebrate the plentiful harvest of corn that had saved them from starvation.

It was quite a shindig. The Pilgrim women, assisted by the children, prepared food for nearly one hundred and fifty people, including a whopping guest list of ninety-one Indian braves. The Pilgrim soldiers marched in full military regalia, against a thunderous chorus of blasting muskets and trumpeting bugles. Both the Indians and Pilgrims held racing and jumping competitions.

To many of us, this may seem like a celebration of thanks. To the Pilgrims, however, a true day of thanksgiving was a sacred time devoted to prayers and fasting. The devout Pilgrims would never have engaged in sports and competitions on a day of thanks, as they did during those fall days in 1621.

That first Pilgrim harvest festival was a secular, or non-church-related, celebration, with eating and rustic games on the menu—nothing else.

In other words, except for saying grace before eating, the Pilgrims did not include a religious service as part of their 1621 celebration.

The first official Pilgrim thanksgiving was celebrated on July 30, 1623. Two years after the Pilgrims' harvest festival in 1621, a drought occurred that lasted from May until the middle of July. The crops withered, and the colonists faced starvation. Governor Bradford ordered a day of prayer, and the Pilgrims prayed for some nine hours, after which the rain fell and the crops were saved.

In gratitude, the governor set aside July 30, 1623, as a day of thanksgiving. Unlike the 1621 festival, the Pilgrims dedicated this day entirely to prayer, with no feasting and games.

It is this thanksgiving observance in 1623, rather than the 1621 harvest festival, that some authorities believe forms the basis for our traditional Thanksgiving holiday. Others suggest it is a combination of both events. For most Americans today, Thanksgiving continues to represent a mingling of the festive with the reverent.

Thursday

The history of the word *Thursday*, the fifth day of the week, is based on Norse, or Scandinavian, mythology.

Thor, considered man's best protector, was the most widely worshiped of the Scandinavian gods. Driving a chariot drawn by male goats, the red-haired and robust Thor wielded his most prized possessions: a magic hammer, iron gloves, and his famous belt of strength. So powerful was Thor that when his chariot rolled, the thunder pealed.

Thor's father was Odin, chief of the gods; his mother was Frigga, from whose name we get *Friday*. The Old Norse *Thor* evolved in Old English as *Thunor*, or *Thur*, which later became *Thunor's Day*, or *Thor's Day*, then *Thurs-doeg*, and finally *Thursday*.

Thanksgiving has been celebrated on the last Thursday of November since 1864, in accord with President Abraham Lincoln's (1809–1865) proclamation of October 3, 1863. This proclamation came about largely thanks to the efforts of a women's magazine editor named Sarah Josepha Hale.

Beginning in 1827, Mrs. Hale doggedly petitioned presidents and government officials to make Thanksgiving Day a national holiday. Finally, in December 1941, a Congressional Joint Resolution specified that the holiday be permanently set on the fourth Thursday in November.

 Do You Know

Not everyone in the United States recognizes the last Thursday in November as Thanksgiving Day. For over two hundred and fifty years, a religious sect known as the Schwenkfelders have observed Thanksgiving on September 24. In the early 1730s, these followers of the German religious reformer Martin Luther (1483–1546) left Germany, where their beliefs were not tolerated, and emigrated to Philadelphia. On September 24, 1734, the Schwenkfelders commemorated their first Thanksgiving with a meal of bread, water, and apple butter. Today on September 24, the sect continues this tradition by eating freshly baked wheat bread spread with their best apple butter.

Canadians celebrate their Thanksgiving Day on the second Monday in October, while people in Japan mark their observance during the first week in November.

November

The Latin word *November*, which means "nine," is the root of November, the eleventh month of the year. When the Romans set up the first calendar, there were only ten months, and November was the ninth.

November days tend to be dreary, so we find few, if any, poets singing the month's praises. In fact, the adjective *Novemberish* has come to denote "dismal and gloomy." In his narrative poem *Enoch Arden*, about a sailor, the English poet Alfred Lord Tennyson (1809–1892) describes "The chill November dawns and dewy-glooming downs." Tennyson could just as easily have been describing the mood of the Pilgrims when they landed on Cape Cod in 1620.

This passage from Governor William Bradford's *Of Plymouth Plantation* reflects their feelings: "What could they see but a hideous and desolate wilderness, full of wild beasts and wild men . . . for summer being done, all things stand upon them with a weatherbeaten face, and the whole country, full of woods and thickets, represented a wild and savage hue."

Harvest

The Old English word for *harvest* is *haerfest*, from the German word *herbst*, which means "the season in which crops ripen"—specifically, the third quarter of the year. Originally harvest applied only to the practice of gathering crops in the fall. Over the years, the word's usage expanded, so that we now harvest a crop at any time of the year. Harry harvests his asparagus stalks in the spring, vine-ripe tomatoes in the summer, and his squash crop in the fall.

As some experts believe, the Thanksgiving Day celebration we traditionally observe in America is based on a Pilgrim harvest festival that was held in the fall of 1621. For centuries in England, people observed "harvest home" celebrations as a way of giving thanks for their crop yields, and the Pilgrims were familiar with this tradition.

Greek and Roman harvest festivals were elaborate affairs, during which participants sang, danced, offered sacrifices to the gods, and gorged on fantastic meals. The Anglo-Saxons, German people who invaded England in the fifth century

A.D. and ruled until 1066, held their harvest home festivities in the fall after the last of the grain had been brought in from the fields. All the workers received a hearty supper and toasted the master and mistress with ale.

Thanks to early seventeenth-century journals, diaries, and letters, we know that the Pilgrim harvest festival in 1621 lasted for three days and was held some time between September 21 and November 9. Much of what we know about this early celebration comes from two major sources: *Of Plymouth Plantation*, the journal of William Bradford, the second governor of Plymouth Colony; and *Mourt's Relation, A Journal of the Pilgrims at Plymouth*, a book written by several colonists. In *Of Plymouth Plantation*, Governor Bradford recounts a letter written in December 1621 by colonist Edward Winslow to a friend in England. This is believed to be the first written description of the Pilgrim harvest festival.

> Our harvest being gotten in, our governor sent four men on fowling, that so we might after a special manner rejoice together after we had gathered the fruit of our labors. They four in one day killed as much fowl as, with a little help beside, served the company almost a week. At which time, amongst other recreations, we exercised our arms, many of the Indians coming amongst us, and among the rest their greatest king Massasoit, which some ninety men, whom for three days we entertained and feasted. . . .

xxxxxxxx Happy Harvest Happenings xxxxxxxx

Studies of folklore and primitive religions indicate a strong similarity among harvest festivals throughout the world. Below are a few examples from the past and present.

ORIGIN/NAME	TIME	CELEBRATES
Biblical Canaan/ *Feast of Tabernacles (Sukkoth)	Fall	harvest/thanksgiving

For centuries Jewish people have gathered together to give thanks for their bounty and remember a time when, with no settled home, they lived in booths, or tents. A symbolic booth is often built as part of the eight-day harvest festival.

Ancient Greece/ Thesmophoria	November	Demeter, goddess of corn

A nine-day festival, in which married women walk to Demeter's temple to offer the goddess fruit and sacrifices.

Ancient Rome/ Ceralia	October	Ceres, fertility goddess

Romans offer Ceres a sow and the first harvest cuttings, then celebrate with music, singing, and food.

New York Iroquois/ Green Corn Festival	October	vegetable harvest

This festival celebrates the harvesting of the Iroquois' staple foods—corn, beans, and squash—with singing, dancing, and a peach-stone dice game.

Germany/ Harvest Festival Erntedankfest	September	harvest

Workers walk through fields singing and make a wreath of wheat and field flowers to present to the owner, who invites them to a feast.

Ancient Mexico	October	harvest

Aztecs behead a young girl who represents Xilonen, the goddess of the new corn.

China/ *Harvest Moon Festival	eighth month of Chinese lunar calendar	autumn moon

One-day festival during which foods are prepared in moon shapes to honor the moon. Especially popular are "moon cakes," lotus seeds encased in dough and set with a preserved duck-egg yolk in the middle. (Look for moon cakes in Chinese bakeries [popular year-round] if you live near a Chinese shopping area.)

India/ *Feast of Lights (Diwali)	October 18	harvest

Hindus place oil lights in windows, along roads, and floating on the Ganges River to guide the goddess of prosperity to their lands.

Great Britain	October	harvest

Harvesters fashion a dressed-up "baby" from the last sheaf of grain and carry it on a pole, singing and dancing, to the barn, where they eat supper.

⋙⋙⋙⋙ *indicates a harvest festival still celebrated today.* ⋙⋙⋙⋙

Fall

Have you ever taken a drive in the county in the fall, hoping to see the brilliantly colored crimson, gold, and orange leaves? If your timing is right, you'll catch the leaves while they are still on the trees, before a windy storm sends them falling to the ground.

The word *fall* developed from the Old English word *feallan* to Middle English *fallen*, which is related to the Old High German *fallan*, all meaning "to drop down from a height." The time when leaves drop down from the trees is called fall in this country. In early England, this period was known as "fall of the leaf." Later, the term was shortened to "fall."

Another word for *fall* is *autumn*, from Latin *autumnus*. Autumn includes September, October, and November, or the period from the September equinox to the December solstice.

In addition to leaves falling in the fall, there are many phrases that incorporate fall and many ways to fall. For example, you can fall into the wrong hands, from grace, in love, or on your knees. Can you add to this sentence? Priscilla had a falling out with her father on a crisp fall afternoon, then fell upon some bad luck when she took a fall from her horse, Skyscraper, near Fallingwater Falls.

Tradition

The word *tradition* evolved from the Old French word *tradicion* or Latin *traditio*, meaning "the practice of handing down a belief or practice." In English poet and dramatist William Shakespeare's (1564–1616) *Richard II* (act III, scene 2, lines 172–3) Richard tells his advisers, "With solemn reverence: throw away respect, tradition, form, and ceremonious duty. . . ."

Celebrating Thanksgiving is a time-honored American custom. But despite two celebrations, held two years apart, there is no evidence to suggest that the Pilgrims observed a regular Thanksgiving in following years. In fact, the history of the Thanksgiving Day tradition in the United States is as rocky as the *Mayflower* crossing.

For one hundred and fifty years after the Pilgrim Thanksgiving of 1623, official days of thanks were observed regionally but not nationally. In 1777, General George Washington (1732–1799) proposed a national holiday that would combine harvest home with a more formal day of giving thanks, but the idea did not gain widespread support. Later, in 1789, the year of his inauguration, President Washington issued the first national Thanksgiving proclamation, setting aside November 26 as the holiday. But, again, his proclamation lacked popular support.

Nine years later, President John Adams (1735–1826) designated May 9, 1798, as a time for "solemn humiliation, fasting and prayer," which doesn't sound at all reminiscent of the Pilgrims' first three-day harvest bash! President Thomas Jefferson (1743–1826) believed that proclaiming a national Thanksgiving holiday would represent a "monarchical practice," so he actively opposed instituting the holiday during his two terms in office. Finally, President James Madison (1751–1836) restored the observance of Thanksgiving on April 13, 1815.

Then another snag. For forty-seven years after President Madison's proclamation, there was no official Thanksgiving Day in this country. As we've read, the tradition was reestablished only after Sarah Josepha Hale's forty-year campaign finally brought results. In 1863, with the Civil War still raging, President Lincoln issued not one but two Thanksgiving proclamations, one for August 6 and a second for the last Thursday of November. The observance may have caught on this time because the country wanted to heal the divisive wounds of the five-year Civil War, which ended in 1865.

Set sail!
English PURITANS become PILGRIMS
and cross the OCEAN
in the *MAYFLOWER*
to WORSHIP in FREEDOM.

Puritan

The Latin words *purus*, "pure," and later *puritas*, "purity," form the root of the word *Puritan*. In mid-sixteenth-century French, the word became *puritan*.

In the purest sense, Puritan refers to a Protestant reformer who wanted to "purify," or reform, the Church of England. In those days, Puritans were regarded as strict, prudish, narrow-minded people, who wore plain clothes and observed the highest moral standards.

Today, when we say someone is a Puritan or puritanical, it usually means they resemble the Puritans in their severe manner or dress—or both. The English novelist G.P.R. James (1799–1860) used the word this way when portraying a character in his book *Arrah Neil*: "His master was a rigid man, a Puritan of the most severe cast."

The Puritan movement took firm hold in England during the period 1560–1660, primarily at the time of Queen Elizabeth I (1533–1603). The Puritans considered the Bible "the pure word of God" and rejected anything that was not contained in the scriptures. This meant that all priests, bishops, and Catholic rituals were looked upon as corruptive influences, since they are not mentioned in the Bible.

 **Do You Know**

The movement of Puritanism was part of the ongoing Protestant Reformation, which began during the reign of King Henry VIII (1491–1547). In 1531, King Henry officially broke ties with the pope in Rome and proclaimed himself supreme head of the church. The monarch severed ties with Rome because the pope had refused to grant him a divorce from his first wife, Catherine of Aragon (1485–1536). After making himself head of the church, the king declared himself divorced. He then married Anne Boleyn (1507?–1536), the second of his six wives, three of whom were named Catherine.

Pilgrim

Those Separatists who sailed to New England in the early seventeenth century were called Pilgrims. The Latin root of *pilgrim* is *peregrinus*, which referred to anyone who came from foreign parts, like the Pilgrims. From it we get the Old French word *pelegrin*. In Middle English the word *pelegrin* traveled from *pelegrin* to *pilegrim* and finally to *pilgrim*.

The Pilgrims who settled in Plymouth came from small congregations in the English Midlands, including one at Scrooby. An active member of the Scrooby congregation was William Bradford, Plymouth's second governor. And it was William Bradford who, quite unintentionally, gave the English Separatists the name Pilgrims.

As the group prepared to leave Holland for the New World, Bradford wrote, "So they left that goodly and pleasant city which had been their resting place near twelve years; but they knew they were pilgrims, and looked not much on those things, but lift up their eyes to the heavens, their dearest country, and quieted their spirits." His words were inspired by New Testament Hebrews 11:13–16, which says, in part, "They were strangers and pilgrims on the earth. For they that say such things declare plainly that they seek a country."

American clergyman Cotton Mather (1663–1728) repeated the word *Pilgrim* when referring to these travelers from Scrooby, and it soon became a familiar term in New England. Later, the word applied to other early Puritan settlers in New England as well.

The Scrooby Pilgrims traveled to a new land in search of religious freedom. Over the centuries, millions of pilgrims have made long journeys, called pilgrimages, to visit shrines or sacred places. In Canterbury, England, Catholic pilgrims traveled to the shrine of Saint Thomas Becket (c. 1118–1170), an archbishop of Canterbury, who was murdered in his cathedral by knights of King Henry II (1133–1189).

According to the tenets of Islam, the religion of the prophet Muhammed, whose name in Arabic means "the praised one," Muslims are expected to make at least one pilgrimage to the holy city of Mecca. A Muslim pilgrimage is known as a hajj. When Muslims complete a hajj, they are addressed as hajji.

Other cities still visited by religious pilgrims today include Fatima, in central Portugal, and Santiago de Compostela, in northwest Spain, where in the Middle Ages two million Europeans made pilgrimages. Do you know of any other destinations for pilgrims today?

Separatists

Some Puritans grew impatient with the slow pace of reforms under Queen Elizabeth I. This group broke away from the Church of England and formed their own congregations in order that they could then worship as they pleased. These Protestants became known as *Separatists* because they had separated from the main church. Puritans, on the other hand, stayed within the church and worked to make improvements.

The word *separate* evolved from the Latin *separare*, "to set apart." Those Puritan Separatists who set themselves apart from the Church of England were considered radical revolutionaries. As a result, both Queen Elizabeth I and her successor, King James I (1566–1625), considered Separatists enemies of the Crown. Some Separatists were executed and jailed; others lost their jobs and were spied on. King James threatened to run all Separatist dissenters out of the country unless they conformed. Hundreds, among them the *Mayflower* Separatists, fled to Holland, a welcome haven for religious dissenters.

The terms *Puritan*, *Pilgrim*, and *Separatist* are sometimes used interchangeably, even though there are differences, as we have seen. Remember, most Puritans were not Separatists but rather remained in the Church of England. The Separatists who colonized New England became known as Pilgrims.

Ocean

From Greek *okeanos* and Latin *oceanus,* "great river or stream," the word became *occean* in both Middle English and Old French. At the time of the Greek poet Homer, around the mid-ninth century B.C., *Okeanos* was called the "great river." Believing this huge river encircled the earth, the Greeks gave it the status of a god. Okeanos was the son of heaven (Uranus) and earth (Gaia).

In 1620, the Pilgrims crossed the North Atlantic, one of the world's most unpredictable and dangerous bodies of water. Had they set sail in August as they had planned, the crossing would have been much smoother. But, owing to one delay after another, the Pilgrims were forced to brave the ocean in the fall, in a ship that carried far too many passengers and provisions for its size.

From *Of Plymouth Plantation,* we know that the over-burdened *Mayflower* encountered fierce gales and storms on its voyage to the New World. The pumps never stopped pumping out seawater. The ship's main beam buckled and cracked but was righted by a "great screw" that one of the Pilgrims had brought from Holland. One passenger was swept overboard, "yet he held his hold, though sundry fathoms under water," and was miraculously rescued. How deep did John Howland go before someone hauled him in with a boat hook? No one knows for sure, but bear in mind that one fathom equals six feet and poor John floundered in unknown fathoms.

The *Mayflower*'s passage across the North Atlantic took twice as long as expected, owing to the weather and winds. Nearly everyone aboard was seasick. The Pilgrims' diet consisted mostly of dried food. Any cooked food was prepared on a little brick oven or on charcoal stoves. Each person had a space approximately six feet by three feet for sleeping. To ease the overcrowded conditions, some passengers slept in the two smaller boats on board: the longboat, an oared boat, and the shallop, a thirty-foot-long sailboat. Others may even have slept on the open deck. Seawater leaking through the ship's seams soaked the passengers' bedding and possessions. Before land was sighted, two people had died: a crew member and one of the young servants, and a baby, appropriately named Oceanus, was born.

 **Do You Know**

Transoceanic voyages to the New World often proved very profitable for investors. In 1619, one English ship sold its cargo of New England fish and furs for nearly five thousand dollars. A typical sailor's pay for such a trip was thirty-three dollars. The Pilgrims got financial backing for their venture from a group of seventy London businessmen interested in turning a profit. In return, these businessmen expected the colonists to repay their investment by sending back furs, timber, and fish from the Hudson River area, their original destination. In the fall of 1621, the ship *Fortune* set out from Plymouth carrying the Pilgrims' first export cargo of beaver skins, sassafras, and timber. But the ship was overtaken by a French man-of-war and the cargo confiscated.

To the Pilgrims, a *fathom* was the spread of a man's arms, or six feet. Here's a list of other old colonial words and their meanings. Some of them you may recognize.

ado	commotion	hart	deer
anon	immediately	league	about three miles
beck	stream	neat	cow
betimes	early	piece	gun
broach	spit for roasting meat	seat	settle
ell	almost four feet (or over a half fathom, right?)	truck	trade
		plain	level
furlong	eighth of a mile (length of a plowed furrow)	let	hinder
		seethe	boil

Mayflower

The famous vessel that brought the Pilgrims to New England was, of course, the *Mayflower*, from the Latin word for May, *Maius*, a Roman goddess, plus Old French *flor*, "flower."

The word *vessel*, which had its beginnings in the Late Latin *vascellum*, "small vase," and later *vaissele* in Old French, has a variety of meanings, including "pots and pans." Structures that hold people and goods (like the *Mayflower*) are *vessels*. Some smaller vessels, such as pots and pans, hold liquids and food. In an 1893 household glossary we find "To wash up the vessel is to clean plates, dishes, etc." Also, blood vessels and arteries in our bodies carry life-sustaining fluids. So vessels can hold or carry objects or liquids. As Lucinda dried the dinner vessels, she received the news that Uncle Sebastian's blood vessel had ruptured while boarding the vessel *Lusitania*.

The Holland Pilgrims began their journey to the New World by boarding the small ship *Speedwell* at the port city of Deftshaven, Holland, on July 22, 1620. They reached Southampton, England, on July 26, where they met the larger ship, the *Mayflower*, with its London passengers. On August 5, the *Speedwell* and the *Mayflower* left Southampton together, but not before officials had demanded nearly one hundred English pounds (about one hundred and sixty dollars today) to clear the harbor. To meet these charges, "some three or four-score firkins of butter" (3360 to 4720 pounds) had to be sold.

The *Speedwell* proved to be as leaky as a sieve, and after two unsuccessful attempts to repair it at the English ports of Dartmouth and Plymouth, the vessel was declared unseaworthy. Those people from the *Speedwell* who decided to continue the trip crowded aboard the already-packed *Mayflower*. It must have seemed an endless voyage for the passengers, considering it was nearly fifty days before they left Plymouth, England, more than two months on the North

Atlantic crossing, and another four months before the last passengers went ashore at Plymouth, Massachusetts.

During the voyage, the passengers divided themselves into two distinct groups. There were the religious Separatists from Holland and a group comprised primarily of soldiers, servants, and artisans, who had left England in search of new economic opportunities. William Bradford called the Holland contingent "saints," to set them apart from those passengers recruited in London by the merchant businessmen. Bradford meant *saint* in the sense of a devout church member, not a saint canonized by the Catholic Church. Anyone not a saint was called a "stranger." Tempers flared between the two groups, especially when the continual psalm singing of the saints got on the nerves of the strangers. Surprisingly, three of the most famous names in Pilgrim history—Miles Standish, Priscilla Mullins, and John Alden —were all strangers.

Mayflower Specifics

TYPE OF VESSEL: three-masted, double-decked, galleon-style ship, 106½ feet long (about a third the length of a football field)

CAPTAIN: Christopher Jones

AVERAGE SPEED: 2 miles per hour, or about 53 miles a day.

DISTANCE COVERED: 3,500 nautical miles

DAYS AT SEA: 66

PASSENGERS: total 102 (50 men, 20 women, 32 children); of total, 41 Pilgrim "saints" (17 men, 10 women, 14 children)

CREW: around 25

PROVISIONS: salt beef and pork, dried salt cod, smoked herring, cheese, lemons, hardtack (saltless hard biscuit), dried peas and beans, sauerkraut, onions, turnips, parsnips, casks of beer, water, and aqua vitae (brandy)

ANIMALS: definitely two dogs (a spaniel and mastiff), and probably several chickens, goats, and hogs

The *Mayflower* Passenger List, 1620
Arranged alphabetically by family

John Alden
Isaac Allerton
Mary Allerton
Bartholomew Allerton
Mary Allerton
Remember Allerton
John Allerton
John Billington
Eleanor Billington
Francis Billington
John Billington
William Bradford
Dorothy May Bradford
   drowned off Mayflower
William Brewster
Mary Brewster
Love Brewster
Wrestling Brewster
Richard Britteridge
Peter Brown
William Butten
   died during crossing
Robert Cartier
John Carver
Katherine Carver
James Chilton
Susanna Chilton
Mary Chilton

Richard Clarke
Francis Cooke
John Cooke
Humility Cooper
John Crackston
John Crackston
Edward Doty
Francis Eaton
Sarah Eaton
Samuel Eaton
? Ely
Thomas English
Moses Fletcher
Edward Fuller
Ann Fuller
Samuel Fuller
Samuel Fuller
Richard Gardiner
John Goodman
William Holbeck
John Hooke
Stephen Hopkins
Elizabeth Hopkins
Giles Hopkins
Constance Hopkins
Damaris Hopkins
Oceanus Hopkins
   born during voyage

John Howland
John Langmore
William Latham
Edward Leister
Edmund Margeson
Christopher Martin
Marie Martin
Desire Minter
Elinor More
Jasper More
Richard More
Mary More
William Mullins
Alice Mullins
Joseph Mullins
Priscilla Mullins
Degory Priest
Solomon Prower
John Rigdale
Alice Rigdale
Thomas Rogers
Joseph Rogers
Henry Sampson
George Soule
Miles Standish
Rose Standish
Elias Story
Edward Thompson
  died on the Mayflower
Edward Tilley
Agnes Tilley
John Tilley

Joan Tilley
Elizabeth Tilley
Thomas Tinker
William Trevore
John Turner
Master Richard Warren
William White
Susanna White
Peregrine White
Resolved White
Roger Wilder
Thomas Williams
Edward Winslow
Elizabeth Winslow
Gilbert Winslow

Most popular names:

John (15)   Mary (5)
William (8)   Elizabeth (3)
Edward (6)
Richard (5)
Thomas (4)

Most unusual names:

Remember, Love, Humility, Oceanus,
Resolved, Wrestling, Peregrine

Worship

Weorth, "worthy," and *scipen*, "to shape," give us the Old English word *weorthscipe*. In Middle English *weorthscipe* became *worshipe*. When most of us think of *worship*, it's probably in the context of paying homage to a divine being in a holy place.

But up through the nineteenth century, the word was often combined with "your" or "his" when referring to a respected person held in honor and esteem. In 1861, you might have addressed a letter this way: To His Worship P. E. Walton, Esq., Mayor of Plymouth. Poet Alfred Lord Tennyson had honor in mind when, in the nineteenth century, he wrote these lines in his poem "Elaine": "It will be to your worship, as my knight . . . To see that she be buried worshipfully."

Writers have also used *worship* to mean "to adore." One of our most popular phrases comes from English novelist Charles Dickens's (1812–1870) novel *Hard Times*, when the charming but egotistical James Harthouse pronounces, "There are ladies—born ladies . . . who next to worship the ground I walk on."

The Pilgrims left England so they would be able to conduct their worship services as they saw fit. Like all Puritans, they wanted to return to a more "pure" form of religion in which there was a direct and intimate contact between man and God. Governor Bradford described their belief as "the simplicity of the gospel, without the mixture of men's inventions."

The Pilgrims based many of their principles on the beliefs of French theologian John Calvin (1509–1564), a Protestant reformer. Among Calvin's doctrines are those that specify that church services be in the vernacular (local language or dialect) instead of Latin, that sermons form a major part of the service, and that all church officers be democratically elected by the people.

Because the Pilgrims rejected Christmas and Easter, these days were just like any other in Plymouth. The customs and rituals we associate with Christmas and Easter would have been considered pagan frivolities to the Pilgrims, punishable by strict penalties. In fact, it was on Christmas Day in 1620 that the Pilgrims, to snub their noses at what they called a "popish festival," began the construction of the first building in Plymouth. The *Mayflower* crew, on the other hand, opened a keg of beer to celebrate the holiday.

The Pilgrims did observe the Lord's Supper because of its scriptural basis, along with Days of Humiliation and

Thanksgiving. They held two Sunday services and frequently had sermons on Thursdays—or on demand. The Pilgrims did not sing hymns or recite creeds during their sevices. Because they are in the Bible, psalms were allowed and were sung without musical accompaniment by the entire congregation. A visitor to Plymouth Colony in 1627 reported seeing the Pilgrims marching in drumbeat to the Sabbath meeting. Apparently they did not equate the simple beating of a drum with music.

Order of Pilgrim Sunday Service in Plymouth

MORNING

Prayer
Scripture
Psalms
Sermon
Sacraments (only after 1629,
    when a minister arrived)
Prayer
Blessing
Church business

AFTERNOON

Prayer
Sermon
Prophesy (readings
    and discussions
    by worshipers)
Offering
Prayer
Blessing
Church business

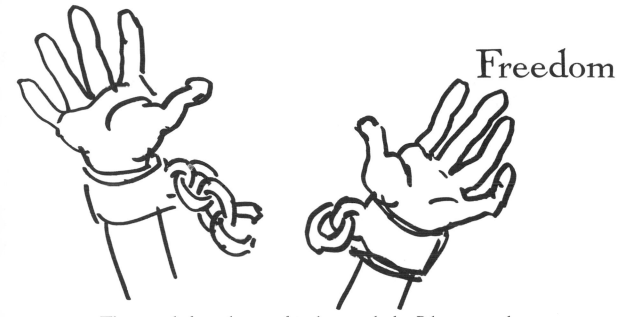

Freedom

The search for religious freedom took the Pilgrims to the wilds of New England. The search for the roots of the word *freedom* takes us to the Old English word *freo*, "free from bondage," plus *dom*, "the state or fact of being," or *freodom*, as it was written before the eleventh century.

Nearly two hundred years after the Pilgrims were denied their religious freedom in England, English poet Lord Byron (1788–1824) wrote "The Prisoner of Chillon." Inspired by a true incident, the poem tells of three brothers imprisoned in a Swiss dungeon for their religious convictions. Two of the brothers die, and they are buried under the floor of the cell. When the surviving brother is finally released, he reflects on the emptiness of his newfound freedom: "My very chains and I grew friends/So much a long communion tends/To make up what we are—even I/Regain'd my freedom with a sigh."

The journey to freedom forced many Separatists to give up their English homes and flee in secrecy to the Low Countries, especially to Holland, where religious tolerance was freely practiced. By 1619, over five hundred Separatists lived in Amsterdam. The Plymouth Pilgrims settled first in Amsterdam, then in a small town called Leyden. The Pilgrims must have felt liberated in their adopted home. Reform literature burned in England was openly published in Holland, and the immigrants had total freedom to conduct their religious services as they wished. Why, then, did the Separatists abandon their newfound freedoms in Holland?

There were a number of reasons. For one, the Pilgrims had trouble learning the Dutch language. Also, because they were not skilled, the men competed for low-paying jobs or as apprentices to blacksmiths, tailors, masons, and weavers. Finally, the Pilgrims were worried about the Dutch influence on their language and religion. They wanted their children to become English rather than Dutch Protestants. And they did not want their children exposed to the temptations of the city. So they opted for a new life in the New World.

 **Do You Know**

Perhaps it is a bit ironic that most of the eighteen servants who came over on the *Mayflower* belonged to the Pilgrim "saints." These servants were indentured, or bound, to their owners for seven years. As a result, these servants performed the most difficult work with no salary. Some of the servants were skilled; others probably came from London's poorhouses.

Early indentures were a kind of special parchment contract designed so that, when ripped in two equal halves, the edges became ragged, or *indented*, from the Latin *dent*, "tooth." Each party kept one half, and any subsequent authenticity questions were settled by matching the jagged teeth of the two halves.

President Franklin D. Roosevelt put forth the notion of four freedoms in 1941 when he said in a speech, "In the future days . . . we look forward to a world founded upon four essential human freedoms. The first is freedom of speech and expression. . . . The second is freedom of every person to worship God in his own way. . . . The third is freedom from want. . . . The fourth is freedom from fear."

Land ho! CAPE COD!
The Pilgrims EXPLORE, armed with MUSKETS,
finally LANDING
on a ROCK in Plymouth.

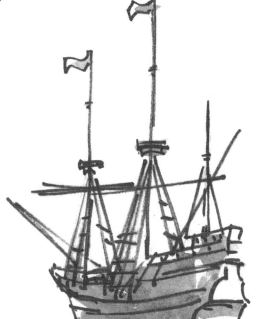

Cape Cod

Dawn, November 19, 1620. After sixty-six grueling, storm-swept days at sea, cries of excitement pierced the cold, blustery air from the deck of the *Mayflower*. The ship's look-out had sighted the blurry shape of land in the distance. The New World. Cape Cod.

The jutting peninsula of Cape Cod was named in 1602 by Bartholomew Gosnold, believed to be the first European to visit the area. The word *cape* comes from the Latin word *caput*, "head." But the origin of *cod* is unknown, for the name of this popular fish exists only in English. One possibility is that it developed from the Old English word *cod*, which referred to the narrow part of the bag on a fishing net. Our word *coddle*, "to pamper," has this same soothing root. If you took a nap on a cod in fifteenth-century Scotland, you were sleeping on a nice soft pillow, not on a slippery fish.

Over the next decades, the commercial fishing industry grew into a large and profitable one for the Pilgrims. So important was the cod, in particular, that in 1784 the Massachusetts House of Representatives voted to hang a wooden cod in its meeting room.

Mourt's Relation includes this description of the Pilgrims' first encounter with the Cape and its abundant fish, among them cod: "The bay is a most hopeful place . . . in fashion like a sickle or fish-hook . . . innumerable store of fowl and fish; skotc [probably skate], cod, turbot, herring, mussels, crabs, and lobsters . . ."

The writer in *Mourt's Relation* might have found the fish-packed, sickle-shaped bay around Cape Cod a "hopeful place," but not everyone on the *Mayflower* shared this feeling, least of all the so-called strangers, the passengers who'd signed on for economic rather than religious motives. The *patent*, or letter of agreement, that the Pilgrims had secured from the Virginia Company entitled them to settle near the mouth of the Hudson River, around Manhattan Island.

Once Cape Cod was identified, the passengers insisted that Captain Christopher Jones correct his course and sail south to their destination. This he did. But while navigating around the hook of Cape Cod, the *Mayflower* encountered dangerous shoals, or shallow water. So dangerous are the waters off Cape Cod that between 1843 and 1859, some five hundred ships were wrecked off the Cape. Rather than risk running the ship aground, the skipper turned back and anchored in the safety of the harbor.

Everyone—except the strangers—agreed with the captain that heading for shore was the best course. The strangers were worried. They had not come thousands of miles for religious liberty; they wanted to rebuild their lives and make a good living in the New World. Knowing full well the patent the Pilgrims held did not apply as far north as Cape Cod, the strangers threatened to cause trouble once ashore. Several Pilgrim leaders recognized the dangers in these threats and, while anchored overnight, drew up a document designed to end the dissension.

This historic document, the Mayflower Compact, specified that one government would rule the new colony, with all passengers—saints and strangers alike—subject to its laws. The Mayflower Compact is considered by many to be the first charter of human liberty, which framed laws that were for the general good of the colony. Also at this time, the men elected John Carver Plymouth's first governor.

Forty-one of the fifty adult males on the ship signed the document on November 11, two days after sighting land. A woman's vote apparently did not count, for there are no female signatures among the signers. Some authorities believe the order in which the men signed indicates the status they would later assume in the colony. Among the first signatures are many familiar names: John Carver, William Bradford, Edward Winslow, William Brewster, John Alden, and Captain Miles Standish.

 **Do You Know**

The Pilgrims' patent entitled them to settle what was called a "plantation," or farming community, at the mouth of the Hudson River, near the present site of Manhattan. How, then, did the *Mayflower* end up off Cape Cod?

Navigation techniques at the beginning of the seventeenth century were far less advanced than those today, and it was not unusual for a ship crossing the ocean to miss its mark by over two hundred miles. Some suggest that the *Mayflower* was blown off course due to severe weather. Another theory is that the Dutch, who already had a thriving settlement on Manhattan Island and didn't want any competition, had bribed Captain Jones to deliberately land off Cape Cod. But considering that the ship's master tried to correct his course, this idea seems farfetched.

Explore

Faced with the uninviting, bleak, wintery wilderness, the Pilgrims must have felt like the first pioneers to explore the rocky coast of Massachusetts. To explore the root of the word *explore*, we must go back to the Latin word *explorare*, "to search out," which evolved into the French word *explorer*.

Explore has exotic overtones that remind us of risk takers like the movie hero Indiana Jones. But you don't have to trek miles in strange new lands to explore. In fact, you don't have to go outside. Doctors conduct exploratory surgery in hospitals to "search out" the source of physical problems.

T. S. Eliot (1888–1965), the American-born English poet and dramatist, reflected on the contradictions of searching in his whimsical verse in *Old Possum's Book of Practical Cats*, which inspired the popular Broadway musical *Cats*: "We shall not cease from exploration/And the end of all our exploring/Will be to arrive where we started/And know the place for the first time."

In addition to Bartholomew Gosnold's, at least twenty other expeditions had sailed up and down the Massachusetts coast before the Pilgrims ever set foot on Cape Cod. One was in 1524, when the Florentine navigator Giovanni da Verrazano (c.1480–1527) traveled along Cape Cod. It's even believed that two members of the *Mayflower* crew had been part of earlier expeditions to the area.

With the *Mayflower* safely anchored in Provincetown Harbor, the Pilgrims' feisty military leader, Captain Miles Standish, led a series of exploring parties along the coast, looking for a good place to settle. He and his men traveled in a thirty-three-foot-long open boat, propelled by sail or oars, which was stored partially disassembled on the *Mayflower*.

This single-masted sloop was called a *shallop*, probably from the Dutch word *sloep*, meaning "sloop." When the shallop entered Plymouth Harbor for the first time on December 10, 1620, it was turned back by a violent storm that broke both the mast and the rudder. The Pilgrims were forced to take shelter on nearby Clark's Island.

Another shallop with a very different destination appears in "The Lady of Shallot," a celebrated poem by Alfred Lord Tennyson: "The shallop flitteth silken-sailed/Skimming down to Camelot." In contrast, the Pilgrim shallop faced choppy seas, with a raw, blustery wind bending its rugged cloth sails. The Pilgrim poem might have run something like this: "The shallop groaneth canvas-sailed/Pounding seasick Pilgrims down to Plymouth."

Pilgrim Exploration Calendar

SEPTEMBER 6, 1920: *Mayflower* leaves Plymouth, England, after repairs.

NOVEMBER 9: Cape Cod highlands are sighted.

NOVEMBER 11: *Mayflower* anchors in Provincetown Harbor; Mayflower Compact signed; John Carver appointed governor. No wood is left, so Captain Miles Standish takes first exploring party ashore in longboat while shallop is being repaired.

NOVEMBER 28: Thirty-four men under Captain Standish explore coast in shallop.

DECEMBER 10: Shallop brings first party into Plymouth Harbor.

DECEMBER 12: First passengers land at Plymouth.

DECEMBER 16: *Mayflower* sails thirty miles into Plymouth Harbor.

DECEMBER 20: Colonists spend first night in Plymouth.

DECEMBER 25: Pilgrims start to build first dwelling.

JANUARY—MARCH 1621: Construction continues; passengers are ferried to land.

MARCH 21: Last boatland of Pilgrims leaves *Mayflower* for land.

APRIL 5: *Mayflower* sets sail for England.

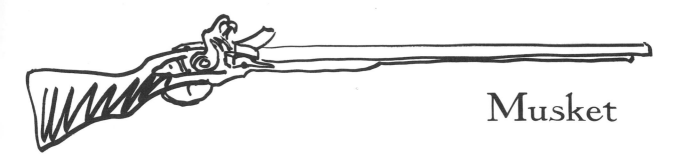

Musket

The origins of the word *musket* go back to the French, who named the weapon after a small hawk called the sparrow hawk. In French, the word *mousquet*—*musket* in English—means "sparrow hawk."

It was very common in the fifteenth and sixteenth centuries to name pieces of artillery after birds of prey and serpents. A *falconet*, after the falcon, was a small cannon, and a *basilisk*, named for a huge legendary serpent with deadly breath, provided the name for a large brass cannon.

Every Pilgrim explorer who went ashore with Captain Miles Standish's first party was well outfitted with offensive arms and protective armor. The musket, used for both warfare and hunting, was the most important. Because of their size and length, about five feet long, muskets inflicted serious wounds and made lots of noise and smoke when fired. Most of them were matchlocks, which means the match, a slow-burning woven cord, had to be kept burning or the gun wouldn't fire. These weapons proved useless in the rain. From *Mourt's Relation*, we read: "In the morning we . . . trimmed our muskets, for few of them would go off because of the wet." In general, the heavy and clumsy matchlock muskets were no match for the lighter, rapid-fire bows and arrows of the Indians.

In addition to their muskets, Captain Standish and his fellow explorers never left the *Mayflower* without their body armor. This originally consisted of an open or closed helmet, breast, back, and thigh plates; it was later simplified to an open helmet and a back and breast plate called a *corselet*. The Pilgrim arsenal also included swords, knives and daggers, pikes (spears on long poles), flint arms, fowling shotguns for hunting, pistols, and cannon.

Did you ever see an illustration of a Pilgrim carrying a short-barreled gun with a flaring muzzle on his shoulder? Called *blunderbusses*, these guns were not developed in Europe until about fifty years *after* the Pilgrims had landed. Since the early Plymouth Pilgrims never had blunderbusses, any artwork depicting this mistake contains an anachronism.

From the Greek *anakhronismos*—*ana*, "back," plus *khronos*, "time"—anachronism is a fancy word for error in time—in the case of a blunderbuss-toting Pilgrim about half a century. If you've ever seen a movie in which the trail of a jet airplane can be seen swooping over a wagon train headed west, you've witnessed a cinematic anachrononism.

Do You Know

Although peace-loving and religious, the Pilgrims had their share of violence, even murder. In June of 1621, two young servants, both in love with a fifteen-year-old young woman named Constance, fought with swords and daggers in Plymouth's first duel. After they had wounded each other, Captain Standish disarmed them, and as punishment, they were strung up with their heads and heels tied together. Taking pity on them, Governor Bradford ordered them cut down after an hour. (P.S.: Constance spurned both and married someone else.)

On September 30, 1630, John Billington, one of the London *Mayflower* recruits, was hanged. He'd been accused of shooting a man who, Billington claimed, interfered with him while he was deer hunting. The Billington family made the headlines again six years later, when John's widow was forced to sit in the stocks for slandering one of the church deacons.

The humiliation of public punishment awaited any colonist who broke the law. Mrs. John Billington's fate was the stocks, a contraption with a low bench and holes to secure extended legs. Here are some other colonial punishments, many of which the Pilgrims used.

51

Curious Colonial Punishments

Pillory: A platform with a framework through which the head and hands were locked. In 1671, a New England politician was exhibited in the pillory for stuffing the ballot box with votes for himself.

Ducking stool: The offender sat on a wooden chair, which was attached to a post set along the bank of a river. The chair was dunked a specific number of times to fit the crime. This device was often used for women accused of slander or for squabbling couples, who were tied back to back.

Scarlet letter: Those found guilty wore an initial around the neck that suggested the offense. For example, those convicted of blasphemy, or showing contempt for God, wore a B. In the novel *The Scarlet Letter*, by American writer Nathaniel Hawthorne (1804–1864), the main character, Hester Prynne, bore an embroidered scarlet *A* on her breast after being accused of adultery.

Branding: Initials were actually branded, or burned, on various—and appropriate—parts of the offender's body. A thief's hand was stamped with a *T*; a person who sold illegal arms to the Indians received a searing *I*.

Whipping post: Offenders were lashed up to forty times, for crimes ranging from shooting a fowl on Sunday to discarding dirty soap suds directly into the street.

Cleft stick: Also known as the gossip's bridge, this contraption consisted of an iron cage that covered the entire head, with a piece of metal that uncomfortably pinched the tongue. Gossiping men and women, in particular, were forced to endure this punishment.

Laying by the heels in the bilboes: A European import, this long, heavy bar featured two sliding shackles that kept the legs raised high in the air while the body rested on the ground.

Landing

From Old High German *lant* and Old Irish *land*, both meaning "open space," evolved the English word *landing*, "the action of coming to land." There are many different kinds of landings. The Pilgrims made a nautical landing off Plymouth. Airplanes make landings on airstrips. The flat part at the bottom of a staircase is also known as a landing. Wilma made a graceful landing when, after leaping down ten steps, she landed on her feet on the stairway landing.

"On Monday (December 12) they sounded the harbor and found it fit for shipping, and marched into the land and found divers cornfields and little running brooks." This description from *Of Plymouth Plantation* is the only eyewitness report of the famous landing of the Pilgrims on Plymouth Rock. This account of the landing took place not from the *Mayflower* (which was still anchored almost thirty miles away in Provincetown) but from the small shallop.

There's been friendly rivalry for years as to which Pilgrim first stepped out of the sloop. Recorded notes give us no clues. Any notion of Pilgrim Mary Chilton being the first out of the shallop is not taken seriously by historians.

Descendants of John Alden claim he was the first. The foundation for both these claims are word-of-mouth stories passed among the Chiltons and Aldens from generation to generation.

We do know for certain that no women were part of the group of thirty-four that first scouted the area. Women and children (and the men not with Captain Standish) stayed behind in the *Mayflower* until the first shelters were ready. Then passengers were ferried across in the shallop. (Even then they had to wade into the icy waters, which contributed further to the later prevalence of pneumonia.) It wasn't until the third week in March that all of the Pilgrims made it to land.

Rock

The solid part of the earth's crust is made of a hard material called *rock*. From the Old French word *roque*, *rock* was adopted in Old English as *rocc*. Rocks come in all sizes, from enormous jagged cliffs to smooth pieces small enough to be skipped across a pond. Other hard objects are also called rocks, like ice cubes, diamonds, and candy.

Since landing on a rock can be a rough experience, the word *rocky* has come to mean hard times. After a rocky day at school, I had two root beers on the rocks and a bag of rock candy. Which is bigger: Plymouth Rock or the diamond Prudence Cape got after a rocky courtship and four marriages that ended up on the rocks? Someone dependable who represents a kind of refuge can be a rock, too. My dog Magic is my rock of sanity at the end of a long, hard day.

Certainly one of the most famous rocks is the one in Plymouth, the rock American poet Henry Wadsworth Longfellow (1807–1882) called "the cornerstone of a nation" in his long narrative poem *The Courtship of Miles Standish*. The actual historic role of this granite cornerstone, however, lacks solid foundation.

We do know from maps and descriptions that there was an enormous boulder about forty feet from shore along the sandy coast in 1620. One document from 1715 referred to it as the "great rock." But since there is no documentation as to exactly where the Pilgrims came ashore, how do we know this rock was a convenient stepping-stone for the Pilgrims?

Let's try to picture that December day when the shallop landed in Plymouth Harbor for the first time. Imagine the small wooden sloop nearing the harbor, probably under sail with a freezing northwest wind bearing down on it. If you

were captain, would you risk damage to your valuable boat by trying to bring the boat alongside a rock so that passengers could step onto it and make for shore? A far more plausible theory is that the Pilgrims used this single huge rock as a landmark to help guide them into the harbor.

Where, then, did this widespread notion of a landing on Plymouth Rock come from? The rock was identified in 1741 by a ninety-five-year-old Plymouth man named John Faunce, a Pilgrim elder. One day after hearing that the town council was considering covering the rock to build a wharf, John hobbled down the hill and announced that his father (who'd arrived in Plymouth three years *after* the Pilgrims) had told him that the rock they were about to bury was "the very place where the forefathers landed." Everyone took Elder Faunce quite literally. And based on this secondhand tale, the chunk of granite known as Plymouth Rock has become one of the most treasured relics in American history.

Inscription on Plymouth Rock

"This spot marks the final resting place of the Pilgrims of the *Mayflower*. . . . They here laid the foundations of a state in which all men for countless ages should have liberty to worship God in their own way. All ye who pass by and see this stone remember, and dedicate yourselves anew to the resolution that you will not rest until this lofty ideal shall have been realized throughout the earth."

 **Do You Know**

Plymouth Rock has long been a symbol of America's freedom. During the Revolutionary War, Plymouth residents took it as a happy omen—not a coincidence—when the rock was split in two while being pried from its bed to use as a pedestal for a liberty pole. And, sure enough, shortly afterward, the colonies officially split from England.

After being pried up and jostled around for a couple of centuries, the two halves of Plymouth Rock were eventually reunited beneath a protective granite canopy at the foot of Coles Hill, where it now sits. Best estimates put the original rock's size at twelve feet in diameter and its weight at seven to eight tons. Over the years the rock has been whittled down in size. Pieces were lost during moves and at the hands of unthinking souvenir hunters who've wanted "a piece of the rock."

If you've ever visited a country fair in the summer, you may have seen Plymouth Rock in one of the exhibit cages in the poultry house. Plymouth Rock is a breed of chicken with a single comb.

SOW and REAP!
COLONY FAMILIES fight to SURVIVE
and invite the INDIANS
to SHARE their BOUNTIFUL CORN.

Sow and Reap

Faced with alarmingly low food supplies in the spring of 1621, the first order of business for the Pilgrims was to sow seeds and, hopefully, reap a harvest. Our word *sow* sprung up from the Old English word *sawan*, "to sow," which developed into Middle English *sowen*.

You can, however, sow more than grain, as we read in Alfred Lord Tennyson's poem "Gardener's Dauphin": "A crowd of hopes,/That sought to sow themselves like winged seeds." You may have heard someone say "You reap what you sow," which is actually paraphrased from New Testament Galatians 6:7, "Be not deceived; God is not mocked: for whatsoever a man soweth, that shall he also reap."

The phrase to "sow one's wild oats" appeared as early as 1576, when a writer named Newton described youth as "that willful and unruly age, which lacketh ripeness and discretion, and (as we say) hath not sowed all their wild oats," in a book titled *Lemnie's Complex*. Because of this phrase, "wild oats" became a name for unsettled young men who sowed wild oats instead of good grain.

We can trace the origins of "feeling one's oats," and "off one's oats" to horses. If you are feeling your oats, you are thought to be as lively as a horse that has just eaten its grain. And when you're off your oats, you've lost your appetite and are not eating well.

Like *sow*, *reap* comes to us from Old English *ripan*, which developed into Middle English *repen*, then *reap*. *Ripan* is also related to our word *ripe*, meaning fully mature. When you reap a harvest, you gather the rewards of what you have previously sown when it is ripe. The Pilgrims brought peas, wheat, and barley from England to plant as their major crops. Unfortunately, the Pilgrims' hopes of reaping a successful harvest in the fall of 1621 were dashed; of the six acres of peas and barley and twenty acres of corn sown, only the corn did well. Reasons for the crop failure are unclear: deteriorated seeds, lack of proper plows, or even poorly timed sowing. One thing is certain: If it weren't for the plentiful corn harvested in the fall, the Pilgrims would have faced certain starvation.

Like *sow*, *reap* does not have to apply to agriculture; you can reap more than just rhubarb. English novelist and journalist Daniel Defoe (1660–1731) wrote of how "the king reaped the fruits of the victory" in his book *Memoirs of a Cavalier*.

The Plymouth settlers at first worked the soil communally, according to the arrangements made with their London backers. Everyone was expected to work in these large common fields, and produce was kept in the common storehouse. In addition, families were given small garden plots to cultivate behind their house. The garden's size was determined by the size of the household.

 **Do You Know**

The English Pilgrims, primarily craftsmen and tradesmen, did not plan to be full-time farmers in New England. John Alden was a cooper (barrel maker), Edward Winslow a printer, and William Bradford a fustian (weaver). But since they'd come from rural English villages, farming was not new to the colonists. As mentioned earlier, the Pilgrims had planned to support their New World venture by exporting valuable fish, lumber, and fur to England. Despite these plans, the Pilgrims lacked the necessary skills and had even failed to bring the right nets and hooks for cod fishing.

Colony

The Pilgrims established their colony, which is "a setlement [sic] in a new country," in Cape Cod. The word *colony* developed from the Latin root *colere*, "to cultivate," which evolved into *colonus*, "farmer," to *colonia*, "farm or settlement."

When the Pilgrim men first explored the land around Plymouth, they found Indian graves and abandoned cornfields. They decided to build their colony on this site for several reasons: The land was already cleared, a nearby hill provided a good fort location, and they were pleased by "a very sweet brook" that ran under the hillside.

By January 9, the common house, the first building in Plymouth, was nearly finished. In addition, each family was busy constructing homes on individual lots. The plot for a family of six measured approximately forty-eight feet by three hundred feet. While awaiting completion of their homes, the colonists spent the greater part of the winter in the twenty-foot-square common house.

To guard against attack, the Pilgrims erected a fort overlooking the colony, which also served as meetinghouse and church. For added security, houses were laid out in rows of two. By June 1621, the weary Pilgrims had managed to complete four public houses and seven private houses.

Representations of Pilgrims living in classic, interlocked log cabins is another historical anachronism. Log cabins were introduced into America by the Swedes, who settled on the lower Delaware River in 1638. Thanks to a letter written by a visitor to Plymouth in 1628, we have this detailed description of how Plymouth Colony looked: "The houses are constructed of clapboards, with gardens also enclosed behind . . . with a stockade against sudden attack; and at the ends of the streets there stood three wooden gates. Upon the hill they have a large square house, with a flat roof, built of thick sawn planks, stayed with oak beams, upon the top of which they have six cannon. . . . The lower part they use for their church."

The Pilgrims left no detailed house plans, but some colonial historians believe that during those early winter months the colonists may have erected crude temporary shelters by bending saplings into a U-shape and covering them with mud. When building their permanent structures, the Pilgrims used an English technique called post-and-beam construction.

First, they erected a framework of large upright logs interwoven with small saplings, then plastered these with a mixture of straw, mud, and clay, which dried hard. Exterior clapboard walls were fashioned from log slabs cut length-wise. The first Pilgrim roofs were made of cattail-reed thatch, but, because of the fire hazard, safer shingles were introduced a few years later.

Inside Pilgrim houses, the dirt or clay floors were laid with rushes. The settlers covered the windows with oiled linen or paper, which admitted precious little light. These houses were considered one and a half rooms, the "half" being a low space under the eaves for sleeping. It was not unusual for as many as eight people to live together in a space the size of today's average living room. About a third of the families had oil lamps and candles; the others made do with the scant light cast from the fieldstone fireplace.

In June 1621, Plymouth Colony boasted seven houses and about fifty residents. By 1624, after the arrival of several ships from England, the colony included one hundred and eighty residents and thirty-two houses.

Family

The word *family* comes from Latin *familia*, "household," from *famulus*, "servant." In Daniel Defoe's *Journal of the Plague Year*, the author combined both early meanings when he wrote, "I was a single man . . . but I had a family of servants."

In zoology and botany, animals and plants that share similar characteristics are grouped together in families. Our next-door neighbors, the Fern family, have a garden devoted solely to plants in the rose family.

The last Thursday in November is traditionally a time when families get together for a celebration of thanks. In his poem "Pumpkin," the poet of rural New England John Greenleaf Whittier (1807–1892) made this observation about such a reunion: "Ah! on Thanksgiving day . . . When the gray-haired New Englander sees round his board/The old broken links of affection restored."

There were a lot of broken links in Pilgrim families by the spring of 1621. Their numbers had been cut in half since the November landing, as four families had been entirely wiped out. During the first winter, unattached people (single men and orphans) joined adopted families and lived in groups. Surprisingly, no young females died during this period, and only three of thirteen young sons perished. Why did the children fare better than their elders? One possible explanation links their survival to the extra food and care they may have received.

With many widows and widowers in the colony during the spring of 1621, it was quite natural that Pilgrim thoughts would turn to rebuilding families. And that meant marriage. Because the Pilgrims did not consider marriage a sacrament of the church, all couples were married by a magistrate, in what we would consider today a civil ceremony. Consequently, a Pilgrim wedding was one of the most festive times in the colony, with plenty of music, singing, and feasting.

The first marriage in Plymouth took place in May 1621, when Governor Bradford married Susanna White and Edward Winslow, both of whom had recently lost spouses. Susanna's second child, Peregrine, was the first Pilgrim baby born after the *Mayflower* anchored off Cape Cod. Several marriages followed, among them that of Governor Bradford, whose first wife, Dorothy, had drowned while the *Mayflower* was at anchor. (Some historians believe she threw herself overboard rather than face the grim prospects of the oncoming winter in a strange land.)

 **Do You Know**

Thanks to Henry Wadsworth Longfellow's celebrated poem *The Courtship of Miles Standish*, Captain Standish, called Captain Shrimp because of his small build, is one of the best-remembered Pilgrims. In the poem, Miles Standish sends a stand-in, John Alden, to court young Priscilla Mullins for him. Priscilla, however, prefers John to the older captain. When the lovers hear of Standish's death, they decide to marry. Just before the wedding, Captain Standish returns and, in a brave act of diplomacy, gives his blessing to them both.

Experts agree that Longfellow was a better poet than accurate interpreter of Pilgrim history, for there is absolutely no evidence to suggest that Priscilla ever caught Miles's eye—or vice versa. Captain Shrimp, a widower, did have a reputation as an impetuous man, so it was no surprise when, after a brief, whirlwind courtship, he married a new arrival named Barbara from the English ship *Anne*. Their marriage took place so quickly that when Barbara's name first appears on Pilgrim records, it's as Mistress Barbara Standish. Her maiden name is lost forever.

To be sure, family life in the Plymouth colony was difficult. A typical workday ran from five in the morning to seven in the evening six days a week during the warm months, and from seven to five in the winter, with a total of two hours off for meals. When children reached the age of seven, they were expected to work with the adults or become apprenticed to a trade.

Because there was no school in Plymouth until 1671, all children were taught at home but only after work was completed. There were few books or supplies. Children learned to read from Bible stories and primers known as *horn books*, so called because the pages were enclosed between thin covers of transparent animal horn.

Given the crowded conditions on the *Mayflower*, the Pilgrims had to leave many of their furnishings and personal belongings behind. As a result, few colonists had the luxury of a bed, a desk, a dining table, or even chairs to sit on while eating. Most families had a chair for the head of the house; others sat on stools, chests, benches, or the floor. Meals were usually laid out on tops of chests or barrels, and many ate standing up.

 **Do You Know**

We often think of the Pilgrims as stern, dour folk who frowned on having fun. True, they took their religion seriously, but they also appreciated good food and drink—and even music, as long as it was *outside* their religious ceremonies.

Another misconception about the Pilgrims relates to their clothing. The popular image is of black or gray clothing with white collars and cuffs, paired with steeple hats and shoes decorated with big buckles. In fact, the early Pilgrims dressed much like a typical rustic of early seventeenth-century England.

This meant that men wore long, loose shirts, knee breeches, stockings, fitted vests called doublets, and brimmed hats. A woman's wardrobe consisted of fitted jackets, skirts, petticoats, large aprons, a cape, and close-fitting caps or hats. Pilgrim clothing was primarily made of wool and linen, with some leather used—and it was not all drab. The colonists made wide use of vegetable dyes in their clothing, especially red, yellow, purple, and green.

And what about those huge, tall, bebuckled Pilgrim hats sported by the Pilgrim men? This was just one of many hat styles. Another popular one was a smaller felt hat with a rounded top and leather band. Whatever the style, there were no ornamental buckles on early Pilgrim hats, shoes, or belts, for buckles were introduced later in the seventeenth century.

Survive

Our word *survive*, "to remain alive after the death of another," has been passed on to us from the Late Latin word *supervivere*—*super*, "over," together with *vivere*, "to live." In Middle French *supervivere* became *survivre*, then *surviven* in Middle English. In addition to a person continuing to exist, objects or events are said to survive as well. Although many Pilgrims did not survive the winter, the memory of their courage will long survive.

Those Pilgrims who managed to "live over" that first bitter winter were left the solemn task of burying the dead. It was not unusual in Plymouth for there to be two or even three funeral processions on the same day. The survival figures speak for themselves: Of the one hundred and two *Mayflower* passengers, fifty died before the following summer. Only five of eighteen wives survived, while ten of twenty-nine servants and single men died. Most Pilgrims died from three primary causes: scurvy, pneumonia, and tuberculosis. The dead were buried on what later became known as Coles Hill and always at night in unmarked graves, because the Pilgrims wanted to conceal their losses from the Indians.

Indian

From the Latin *Indianus*, the "Indus" River, which flows 1,800 miles from Tibet through Pakistan, and French *indien* comes the name *Indian*, specifically referring to the native people of India or the East Indies. Today, however, virtually all aboriginal races of America and the West Indies are considered Indians. Exceptions are the Eskimos and frequently the Patagonians and inhabitants of Tierra del Fuego, off South America.

How these American and West Indian natives got the name *Indian* is the result of a geographical mix-up. We can put the blame squarely at the feet of the Italian navigator Christopher Columbus (c.1451–1506).

When Columbus set out from Spain in 1492, his plan was to reach Asia by sailing west. Because of a geographical error, he instead reached land in the Bahamas, the western world, on October 12. Since he thought he was in Asia, Columbus called the natives he met there "Indians."

There was no official Indian-greeting party to meet Captain Standish and his men when they came into Plymouth Harbor. But they did find signs of the Indians everywhere. One day, drawn to a curious mound of sand, the Pilgrims uncovered and carried away several bushels of the dried corn buried by the Indians for future use. Worse, the Pilgrims removed beads and odd knickknacks from Indian graves.

It wasn't long before the Indians, wary up till now, attacked Standish and his party. Arrows and musket shots were exchanged, with no injuries to either side. One theory is that the Indian attack was a reprisal for the Pilgrims' thefts of corn and trinkets. True or not, this confrontation was the only time in the entire history of Plymouth Colony that the settlers were attacked by the Indians.

The Pilgrims may have expected bows and arrows, but, in fact, they received only help and encouragement from the natives. It is not an exaggeration to say that the Pilgrims owed their very existence that first difficult year to the Indians—especially to two Indians, Samoset and Tisquantum, better known as Squanto.

One March day, while the Pilgrims were in the meetinghouse, they were dumbfounded when a nearly naked Indian calmly marched into the building and greeted them in broken English. The first thing the modest Pilgrims did was throw a long red coat over his scantily clad body.

The Indian, Samoset, told them he'd learned English while living with fishermen off the coast of Maine. Samoset proved invaluable to the colonists by introducing them to Chief Massasoit, head of the influential Wampanoag tribe.

The Pilgrims soon discovered that cementing a relationship with Massasoit would put them on good terms with all the Indian tribes in the region. The peace they signed with Massasoit lasted for many years.

The following month, Samoset returned with another Indian, who spoke even better English. His name was Squanto. Among the various accounts that explain Squanto's fluency, the most valid tells of how he had been sold into slavery in Spain and eventually made his way back to New England via England. He reached Plymouth only to find that all the people in his village of Patuxet, which means "at the little falls," had been killed by a plague, probably introduced by European sailors.

It was Squanto who told the Pilgrims that Plymouth was situated on the very spot where his people had lived and died. So attached was Squanto to the Pilgrims that he never left them, and on his deathbed he asked Governor Bradford to pray that he be admitted to the "English heaven."

Not only did Squanto help the Pilgrims build their houses, but he taught them valuable skills, among these how to catch spawning herring, trap deer and rabbits, and plant corn. The Indian method of planting corn gave the colonists their first successful harvest. Squanto showed them how to fertilize a small hill with three dead fish, then place the corn seeds on top of the hill and cover them.

Share

The root of the word *share* relates to harvest time, coming from the Old English *scieran*, "to cut," from an Old Teutonic word *skaro*, "to cut or divide." In Middle English, it became *schar*. When you say "I want my cut," don't you really mean "I want my fair share"?

Over one thousand years ago a share was the blade of a plow that cuts a trench, or furrow, in the ground in preparation for planting. These blades are called *plowshares*. In making pleas for peace, writers and speakers often quote the familiar words of Isaiah 2:4: "They shall beat their swords into plowshares, and their spears into pruninghooks: nation shall not lift up sword against nation, neither shall they learn war any more."

Another kind of share relates to business. If you have a certificate of ownership representing part of a company's stock, you are said to own shares. Flynn's father told him to beat his sword into a plowshare and do his share around the farm or forfeit all his shares of family stock.

After all the help Samoset and Squanto gave the Pilgrims, it seemed only fitting that the colonists invite them to share in their harvest festival. Just before the celebration, the weekly individual food ration of the Pilgrims was doubled to include an extra peck of corn. The abundance from the twenty acres of corn was divided equally so that everyone got an extra share. The harvest festival was a celebration of this bounty.

In addition to their English-speaking Indian friends Squanto and Samoset, the Pilgrims sent out an invitation to Chief Massasoit. But they were probably a little surprised when the proud chief showed up with ninety of his braves. This put the total head count for three days of harvest sharing at around one hundred and fifty.

How many times have you been told to "share and share alike"? Up until the eighteenth century, the phrase was "share and share like." "Alike" appeared in several later literary references, among them English satirist William Thackeray's (1811–1863) *The Virginians*: "She fondly hoped that he might be inclined to go share and share alike with Twin junior."

Bountiful

Bountiful, "a full state of abundance or generosity," reached English from its Latin root *bonus*, "good." In Old French, *bonus* became *bonte*, which evolved into Middle English *bounte*, "goodness." The suffix *ful*, meaning "characterized by," is from Old English *full*. If something is characterized by goodness, it is said to be bountiful.

We usually associate the word *bountiful* with a fruitful season of the year, like the time of the bountiful fall harvest. Even people can be bountiful. A character introduced in English comic playwright George Farquhar's (1678–1707) *The Beaux' Stratagem* was a very generous woman named Lady Bountiful. Ever since, any highly respected woman who is especially giving is called a "Lady Bountiful," especially in England. Next time you want to thank a generous woman in your neighborhood, address the note to "Lady Bountiful."

A character that sometimes turns up in books or movies set in the Old West is the bounty hunter. These people pursue wanted criminals and bring them in to law officials to collect the posted reward. The notion of a bounty as a reward goes back to the thirteenth century, when it meant a generous gift. Later, in the mid-eighteenth century, the word was expanded to include a reward offered for the capture of animals that threatened livestock or criminals. I'm offering a bounty of five dollars and a bountiful supply of Good & Plenty candy for clearing the swamp of mosquitoes in my backyard. Signed, Lady Jenny Russ.

Thanksgiving meals are usually bountiful, and that first harvest festival in the fall of 1621 was indeed a bountiful one for the Pilgrim settlers. When Governor Bradford sent the men out hunting, they returned with a wide assortment of game and fish, including duck, wood pigeon, goose, eels, lobsters, oysters, clams, wild turkeys, cod, and sea bass. The hunters shot enough fowl to feed the Pilgrims for almost a week. But with nearly one hundred hearty Indian appetites to satisfy, it is doubtful there were any leftovers. Luckily, Massasoit's braves didn't come empty-handed; they contributed five deer to the festivities.

One of *bountiful*'s synonyms, or words with the same meaning, is *plentiful*, from the Latin word *plenus*, "full," and Middle English *plente*. William Shakespeare wittily used *plentiful* in *Hamlet* (act II, scene 2, line 202): "They have a plentiful lack of wit."

Corn

The Old English word *corn* corresponds to Old Norse *korn*, meaning "a grain or seed," as in a *corn* of salt or sand. William Caxton (1422–1491), a translator who became the first printer in England, wrote in *Chronicles of England*, "He offered three corns of incense to the sacrifice of the idols."

Used generally, the term *corn* includes all the cereal grasses, such as wheat, rye, barley, oats, and rice. When applied locally, *corn* is taken to mean the most important cereal grain of that area. In England *corn* is wheat; in Ireland it's oats. In the United States *corn* is, specifically, the grain that grows on the cob enclosed by a husk.

Native to the American continent, corn grows from southern Argentina north to Canada and is one of the most widely planted grains. Since corn was not a major crop in England, the Pilgrims brought no corn with them. The corn introduced to the Pilgrims by the Indians was appropriately called *Indian corn*, later just *corn*. This Indian corn, called *flint*, is not the sweet corn we know today. Our sweet corn is of recent origin. It's thought to be a mutation of the Indian flint corn that the Pilgrims grew. Early sweet corn varieties had short ears (five to seven inches) and white kernels. In 1902, the first yellow variety, called Golden Bantam, was introduced.

In *Letters in New England*, John Winthrop (1588–1649), Puritan governor of Massachusetts Bay Colony, confirmed colonial dependency on the grain: "Though we have not beef and mutton, etc., yet, (God be praised) our Indian corn answers for all."

The Pilgrims harvested an abundant crop of Indian corn, but is there any basis to the popular notion that they snacked on popcorn at the harvest festival? According to one legend, Chief Massasoit's brother contributed several sacks of pre-popped corn. Whether he did or not, experts acknowledge that it was the Indians who discovered the art of popping corn as early as 3,000 B.C. Over four thousand years later, Christopher Columbus bought necklaces of strung popcorn from natives in the West Indies.

Popcorn gets its name from the Middle English word *poppe*, an explosive noise. Since the word *poppe* imitates the sound of something exploding, like popcorn in a pan, it is said to be *onomatopoeic*, from the Greek *onoma*, "name," and *poiein*, "to make." A few examples of onomatopoeic words are *whack, hiss, buzz, gurgle,* and *burp.*

Not all corn, however, will explode. In order for corn to pop, the kernel has to be about 14 percent water, so that

when hot, the water will turn to steam and pop the kernel. Indian flint corn did puff up a bit when dry heated, but not like our fluffy kernels today. The Indians popped their corn by skewering ears of corn onto a stick or scraping the kernels from the cob and throwing them into the flames. In each case, the Indians gathered up the popped kernels that shot out of the fire.

Do You Know

Scorched fingers received a break—and popcorn soared in popularity—when the first electric corn popper was introduced in 1907. But the movie industry was responsible for firmly establishing popcorn's fame. By 1950, over 85 percent of all movie theaters sold popcorn. Today, 192 million pounds of corn are popped annually in the United States, and the average American pops about two pounds of popped corn into his mouth—at home or when he pops in to catch a movie.

A cornucopia—in Latin *cornu copiae*—is literally a "horn of plenty." As a symbol of fruitfulness and abundance, people often place cornucopia baskets on their Thanksgiving tables to symbolize the plentiful harvest. In Greek mythology, the original horn of plenty belonged to a goat that suckled Zeus as an infant.

81

GOBBLE!
CARVE the TURKEY so all can enjoy
this FEAST of STUFFING,
BISQUITS and GRAVY,
JUICY CRANBERRIES, SQUASH,
and PUMPKIN PIE.

Gobble

Did you ever hear someone call a turkey a "gobbler"? The male turkey's fussy-sounding gobbling call has earned him the nickname "gobbler." The word *gobble* is slang of unknown origin, possibly from the Irish word for mouth, *gob*, which suggests the noisy sound made when swallowing. If this is true (try it in private!), this makes *gobble* an onomatopoeic word just like *pop*.

Over the centuries, *gobble* has enjoyed a wide slang usage. Four hundred years ago, if you stuffed your mouth full of food and swallowed it noisily, you were guilty of gobbling it. "The Supper gobbled up in haste, Again afresh to Cards they run," wrote English satirist Jonathan Swift (1667–1745) in his book *A Lady's Journal*.

In a story in the February 1888 issue of *Harper's Magazine*, one of Henry James's characters observed, "I happen to know . . . that the moment Mr. Pringle should propose to my daughter she would gobble him down." In this instance, *gobble* means to seize upon greedily; apparently the young woman was ready to accept without a moment's hesitation.

Did you ever get impatient while sewing or mending a piece of clothing and start taking long stitches to finish faster? Long stitches made too long in a hurry are called "gobble stitches." Have you noticed one characteristic common to the various meanings of *gobble* discussed? They all involve speed.

Here are some other not-so-common slang gobbles:

- a quiet, straight golf putt
  headed straight for the hole
- a mouth
- an overtime shift, especially
  at a printing office

After putting in long hours at the newspaper office, Arnold headed for the golf course. "Shut your gobble, I'm trying to concentrate!" he shouted to the noisy crowd as he sent a gobble right toward the eighteenth hole.

Do You Know

Gobbledygook is descriptive (and fun-to-say) slang for a long, self-important speech or text. First Tom bored us with a lot of gobbledygook, then he gobbled up all the Thanksgiving gobbler.

Carve

The Old English word for *carve*, *ceorfan*, corresponds to the Old Frisian *kerva* and Old High German *kerban*, which means "to notch or carve." In English poet Geoffrey Chaucer's "The Prioress's Tale," one of *The Canterbury Tales*, he describes the slashing of a young man's throat, "There he with throat carved lay."

Today, the notion of carving someone is considered slang usage, as in American detective writer Dashiell Hammett's (1894–1961) novel *The Dain Curse*: "The man . . . stood . . . waiting to carve me when I came out; and my fall had saved me, making him miss me with the blade."

More traditional carvings are culinary ones, in which meat is sliced into serving portions. At American dinner tables, one person is often the designated carver. But when the Pilgrims gathered for their harvest meal, each carved his or her own meat. The diners sat on benches, the ground, or they stood, with the few chairs reserved for the colony leaders, like Governor Bradford and Captain Standish.

The Pilgrims ate from small round or square wooden plates, called *trenchers*, and wooden bowls and cups. Often, two people shared trenchers and bowls, and sometimes even drinking cups.

Except for the highest classes, all people in seventeenth- and eighteenth-century Europe ate from communal bowls and plates. One period etiquette book warns diners, "When everyone is eating from the same dish, you should take care not to put your hand into it before those of higher rank have done so." This would have applied to the Pilgrims. Governor Bradford would have speared his share of carrots before any of the servants helped themselves.

Dinner service consisted of a spoon, knife, and large napkin for each harvest diner. This three-foot-square linen napkin came in handy not only for wiping the mouth, but also for picking up food and holding meat in place while carving, since forks were not available.

Forks, from Latin *furca*, a "farmer's pitchfork," first showed up in Italy in the eleventh century. Looked upon as a novelty for hundreds of years, forks did not come into common use until the eighteenth century, when the French nobility decided they were fashionable.

Turkey

From the Latin *Turc*, later *Turchia*, comes the word *Turkey*, a country in western Asia and southeastern Europe. But how was the largest North American game bird, the symbol of Thanksgiving, named after an exotic country, home to the once-powerful Ottoman Empire, sultans, fez hats, and velvety rugs? It's another case of mistaken geography, similar to the naming of the Indians.

In the sixteenth century, a bird was imported from Africa. These birds were transported through the Turkish Empire and into Europe. Round-shaped birds with featherless heads and dark body feathers speckled white, they were actually guinea fowls. Ignoring the fact that the bird was really native to Africa, the guinea fowl was inappropriately named the turkey.

At about the same time, Spanish *conquistadores* exploring South America returned to Europe with cargoes of a newly discovered large wild bird. Because the tasty bird resembled the guinea fowl, the first error was compounded by calling this new bird a turkey, too. Years later, the guinea fowl was correctly identified and recovered its real name, but the name *turkey* stuck for the native American bird.

In 1524, Henry VIII served up the first South American turkey for his English court. There is little doubt the Pilgrims ate turkey in England; but the question is, did they eat roasted or boiled turkey for Thanksgiving? We know the Pilgrim hunters returned with enough fowl to feed the colony for a week, yet we can only assume that turkey was on the menu.

Whether or not the Pilgrims roasted turkeys on spits in the fall of 1621, the fact remains that the turkey did not become an American Thanksgiving tradition until the 1860s. The bird's place as a Thanksgiving custom was made even more secure after World War II. Then the poultry industry launched a full-scale marketing campaign, which neatly coincided with the introduction of hybrid birds that outweighed their wild cousins.

Turkey has also enjoyed an ongoing tradition in American slang usage. Have you ever heard someone called a "turkey"? It's slang for a worthless person. Don't be a turkey and wolf down all the chicken stew Aunt Bunny made for us. One hundred and fifty years ago, when you "talked turkey" you weren't discussing the holiday bird; you were talking serious business. This phrase supposedly originated in the nineteenth century with an employee of the United States Engineer Department. As the story goes, a white man and an Indian went hunting together for equal shares. When it came

time to divide their bounty of two turkeys and three crows, the white man tried to keep the two turkeys for himself and stick the Indian with the less-tasty crows. At this point, the Indian reportedly replied, "You talk all turkey for you, and only talk crow for Indian."

Here are a few other slang turkeys:

- a theatrical failure
- a victim of an attack
- a fifty-cent piece
- a tramp's bundle (Australia)

to turn turkey—be cowardly

cold turkey—sudden withdrawal from a bad habit

turkey stone—turquoise

We have the Romans to thank for our tradition of snapping a wishbone, with luck going to the person with the bigger half. By the time the Pilgrims came to Cape Cod, the tradition of breaking a wishbone was well established in England. According to popular lore, the Pilgrims brought the custom with them and snapped turkey wishbones during the first harvest festival. Word historians believe our phrase "get a lucky break" originated with this tradition, when applied to the person who gets the bigger half of the bone.

Feast

The origins of the word *feast* are from the Latin *festa*, meaning "festal ceremonies." In the thirteenth century, a feast was a religious anniversary celebrating an important event or person. Notable religious feasts include Catholic saints' days, Jewish Passover, and Easter.

Religious feasts are said to be either movable or immovable. Easter is a movable feast because its date varies every year. Christmas, which is always celebrated December 25, is an immovable feast.

The most popular meaning of *feast* is that of an elaborate meal or entertainment, similar to the one the Pilgrims enjoyed after harvesting their twenty acres of Indian corn. We also say something is a feast if it gives abundant pleasure. The Pilgrims would undoubtedly have shared the sentiments expressed in the poem "Love and Liberty—A Cantata," by Scottish poet Robert Burns (1759–1796): "A fig for those by law protected!/Liberty's a glorious feast!"

Nobody at that famous feast in the fall of 1621 stopped to write down each course, although both *Of Plymouth*

Plantation and *Mourt's Relation* refer to specific foods. Historians can only speculate as to the complete menu, based on what the colonists brought from England, any native plants incorporated, and what the Indians provided.

We know the feast included vegetables. But the word *vegetable* did not exist in the early colonial vocabulary. They called vegetables "sallets." Pilgrim sallets served at the harvest meal included parsnips, carrots, turnips, watercress, onions, radishes, and cabbage.

By the fall of 1621, the Pilgrims' stores of butter, flour, and sugar were all but depleted. Cows did not arrive in Plymouth until four years later, so any milk and cheese would have been supplied by goats, which experts believe were brought over on the *Mayflower*. Tea and coffee, not yet introduced in England, were unknown to the Pilgrims. The Pilgrims brewed red and white wine from abundant wild grapes. The most common drink at the three-day festival was wine.

Considering that the Pilgrims made do with what was available, they had quite a feast. Since there were no courses, all food—from soup to fruit—was placed on the cloth-covered tables at the same time, and everyone helped themselves. Their reach-and-eat style of dining is much less formal than today's "Will you please pass the . . ."

Here is a list of what the Pilgrim women probably served up for the harvest feast. One story has it that Priscilla Mullins was one of the best cooks in the colony and created several delicious harvest dishes. You may be surprised to find missing some of the foods we particularly associate these days with harvest time and Thanksgiving.

ON THE MENU:

cod, sea bass
duck, goose, turkey, swan, pigeon, partridge
cornmeal (hoecakes and ashcakes)
five deer
parsnips, carrots, turnips, onions, cabbage, radishes, beets,
lettuce, boiled pumpkins, squash, leeks
eggs, goat's milk
beer, brandy, gin, wine
boiled unsweetened cranberries
wild currants, raspberries, cherries, beach plums, grapes,
blueberries
Indian flint corn
shellfish (not highly regarded; may have been omitted)
sauces thickened with egg yolk and cornmeal

Stuffing

As a verb, *stuff* has its beginnings as a military word in Middle English *stoffe*, from Old French *estoffer*, "to equip or stock." In the early 1600s, a town outfitted with men was said to be "stuffed" with soldiers.

For over four hundred years, *stuffing* and *stuffed* have implied overindulgence. When you stuff too much turkey into your mouth, you say "No more. I'm stuffed!" whether you eat the stuffing or not.

For their first harvest meal, the Pilgrims cooked all the fowl and deer on a spit, which turned slowly over an open fire. Old colonial cookbooks do contain recipes for stuffings.

Pilgrims called these stuffings "puddings in the belly," a very descriptive term for putting moist ingredients into the cavity of a bird. A typical Pilgrim pudding in the belly was made by combining herbs, hardened egg yolks, grated bread, cream, raisins or currants, sugar, spices, and perhaps nuts.

The question is, did the Pilgrim cooks stuff any wild turkeys they may have had during the celebration? The answer varies, depending on which historical account you read. Some Pilgrim experts think stuffing the turkeys was unlikely, because stuffings do not cook evenly when the fowl is roasted over a spit.

Stuff also turns up in American slang phrases, especially in phrases like "stuffed shirt," a conceited, cautious person; "beat the stuffing out of it," to give an unmercifully hard whipping; and "stuff," a catchall word for an odd collection of items. Before voting, a stuffed shirt named Hathaway packed up his stuff, ate a meal of stuffed grape leaves, stuffed the ballot box, then got the stuffing knocked out of him.

There's also

> stuff and nonsense
> knows his/her stuff
> hot and stuffy

Go ahead and add some of your own stuff!

Biscuits and Gravy

What can equal the smell of biscuits rising golden brown in the oven! The word *biscuit* arose from the Latin word *biscoctum*, "twice-baked bread." From the sixteenth to the eighteenth century, the English word was spelled as it was pronounced, *bisket*. Later, the French spelling, *biscuit*, was adopted, but the English pronunciation (*bisket*) remained.

Perhaps you've heard someone shout "That takes the cake!" This can be interpreted to suggest "What nerve!" or "That's the limit!" A variation, especially in England, is "to take the biscuit." Here's how English comic writer P. G. Wodehouse (1881–1975) put it to work in his droll novel *Very Good, Jeeves!*: "Of all the absolutely foul sights I have ever seen, this book took the biscuit with ridiculous ease."

Because it would be several years before enough wheat was grown in the colonies for flour to be plentiful, it's unlikely the Pilgrims enjoyed warm, tender biscuits. Since corn was abundant, however, the Pilgrims used ground corn as a substitute for flour in making their bread.

The word history of biscuit's culinary mate *gravy* is a fuzzy one. In Middle English, the word appeared as *grauey*, which may have been a misreading of *grave*, a word from French cookbook texts.

If we refer to New England seventeenth-century cookbooks, we see that early colonists thickened their gravies with animal blood, egg yolks, and bread crumbs, with flour gravies adopted later. Both Pilgrim gravies and sauces were so thick they could be considered a cross between our easy-pouring gravy and stuffing. Typical colonial gravy ingredients included beer, salt, fine bread crumbs, hardened egg yolks, meat drippings, and lemon or orange peel, when available.

Like *turkey*, *gravy* has a rich history as a slang word. *Gravy* in popular speech denotes money or praise easily or unexpectedly earned. The *Saturday Evening Post* magazine from July 1901 featured a story with these lines: "Stick him for all you can. You're a hard worker, and you mustn't let somebody else git the gravy."

If you are lucky enough to hitch a ride on the gravy train, you've gotten lucky without much effort. The phrase probably originated from jargon—or language—used by railroad crews in the early 1900s. To them a gravy run or a gravy train was an easy stretch on the train with good pay.

Juicy Cranberries

Juicy comes to us from the Old French and Latin word *jus*, meaning "broth or juice." Over the centuries juicy has been widely used to describe everything from succulent cranberries and a first-rate base hit to the moistlike coloration in a painting to a racy story.

In his novel *David Blaize*, English writer E. F. Benson (1867–1940) noted, "It didn't often happen that the first ball of an inning was slogged for six. Juicy hit, too!" An art critic writing in a newspaper article from 1897 described "a fine bit of juicy landscape and rich color." In *Main Street*, American writer Sinclair Lewis's (1885–1951) acclaimed novel, we read, "The gang . . . gathered in a snickering knot to listen to the 'juicy stories.'"

There are no juicy tales that surround the history of the word *cranberry*, however. Its name was probably adopted by the Pilgrim colonists from the Low German word *kranebere*, "crane-berry," and carried back to England with the imported American berries. Like wild turkeys and corn, the local Cape Cod cranberries were native to America.

Again, there is no direct evidence that links cranberries

to the first harvest menu, but since the fruit grew abundantly, we can assume the cooks used the berries, which were most likely gathered by the children. If so, the cranberries would have been boiled and mashed into sauces to serve with the meats. Missing was the jellied cranberry sauce so familiar to our Thanksgiving tables, owing to the scarcity of sugar. Cranberries may also have been mixed into Pilgrim "puddings in the belly," or stuffing.

 ## Do You Know

Cranberries were harvested in the wild for almost two hundred years after the Pilgrims colonized Cape Cod. The first producer to cultivate cranberries was Henry Hall in 1816. He discovered that the secret to growing large, juicy cranberries was to plant the vines where the sand from the dunes blows over them. Cranberries grow in wet spongy bogs, from the Gaelic word *bogach*, *bog*, "soft." Today's commercial cranberry bog plantations are built on peat swamps.

When in 1677, the independent-minded colonists decided to forge their own pine tree shilling coin, King Charles II was furious. So the Pilgrims shipped over ten barrels of cranberries—a tart, puckery appeasement, indeed!

Squash

A favorite Thanksgiving dish is made from a gourd that grows on a vine-trailing ground plant. It's called squash and is often crushed into pulp, or *squashed*, then baked or boiled and served with butter and brown sugar. The Narragansett Indians, one of the most important tribes in the Cape Cod area, called their squash gourds *asquutasquash*, "that which is eaten raw." Throw out the first seven letters and you get a much-easier-to-say *squash*.

In this country we have many different kinds of squash, among them summer, buttercup, and butternut. From early writings we know that early seventeenth-century squash was quite different from what we buy and grow today. The founder of Providence, Rhode Island, Roger Williams, called squash "vine apples" and said they were about the size of apples and very delicious.

The word *squash* is, like *pop* and *gobble*, onomatopoeic. English novelist Charles Dickens (1812–1870) used squash onomatopoeically in his dramatic novel *A Tale of Two Cities*. If you've ever walked in the mud or had your shoes fill up with water, you'll understand this description of passengers forced to walk up a steep hill beside their coach: "Once more, the Dover mail struggled on, with the Jack-boots of its passengers squashing along by its side."

Another familiar use of *squash* is in squash rackets, the official name of the racket game played against four walls with a long-handled racket and a soft rubber ball. The game was invented at England's Harrow School in 1886. After a fast game of squash, Arthur Vine bought a buttercup squash at the farmers' market, but it was squashed by a passing car when it rolled out of his basket.

 **Do You Know**

If you called someone a *squash* in early seventeenth-century England, you might have ducked to avoid getting hit with a rotten tomato. *Squash* was formerly used as a way of showing contempt, as illustrated in this example from William Shakespeare's comedy *The Winter's Tale* (act 1, scene 2, lines 159–160): "This kernel, this squash, this gentleman."

Pumpkin Pie

According to researchers, the tradition of serving pumpkin pie at Thanksgiving actually preceded turkey as an American holiday staple. But how did the word *pumpkin* become a staple in our language? *Pumpkin* came into English from the Greek word *pepon* and French *pompon*, both meaning "melon." The spelling evolved into *pumpion*, or *pompion*, as the Pilgrims wrote it. The *-kin* was added later in the American colonies.

Like the word *squash*, *pumpkin* has been incorporated into slang usage in this country. An important person or thing is sometimes called "some pumpkins," or "punkins," as in the American writer Jack London's (1876–1916) novel *The Valley of the Moon*: "Say, friend, you're some punkins at a hundred yards dash, ain't you?" Also, anyone with their hair cut short all around or who has a round-shaped head is ripe for being called a "pumpkin-head," which can imply stupidity as well.

A famous literary pumpkin-headed ghost appears in American writer Washington Irving's (1783–1859) "The

Legend of Sleepy Hollow." Can you think of famous pumpkins in other books and stories you may have read? What about Cinderella's coach? Where did Peter put his wandering wife?

Pumpkins grew easily and abundantly around Plymouth, so the bright orange gourd became a vital part of the Pilgrim diet. Yet, lacking the required flour, sugar, or molasses, the Pilgrim cooks were unable to turn out fresh pumpkin pies for that first harvest dinner. Pumpkins were widely used in soups (called pottage), puddings, custards, and, when flour was available, pies. A folk song from 1630 illustrates the Pilgrim dependence on pumpkin:

For pottage and puddings and custards and pies
Our pumpkins and parsnips are common supplies;
We have pumpkin at morning and pumpkin at noon,
If it was not for pumpkin, we should be undone.

 **Do You Know**

Pumpkins are one of the fastest-growing plants known. One man in Missouri grew a vine that measured almost two thousand feet after six months. The winner of the World Pumpkin Federation Contest in October of 1986 in Jacobstown, New Jersey, weighted 671 pounds and measured 11' 11¼".

The word *pie* was first served up in English as a dish of meat or fish, covered with pastry and baked, as early as the mid-1300s. Fruit pies appeared around 1600, with the earliest being the all-American favorite apple. The Latin word *pica* gave us the Old French word *pie*, the same as our English word. *Pie* in English was most likely the same *pie* as in *magpie*, a black-and-white bird with a chattering voice that gathers odd collections of objects. But no one has explained why.

Pie can also suggest something that is appreciated, as in this line from American humorist Mark Twain's (1835–1910) novel *Huckleberry Finn:* "You're always as polite as pie to them." Other informal or slang expressions make use of *pie*, like "easy as pie," referring to jobs that are a cinch. If you "have a finger in the pie," you keep busy at a job. For those who dream rather than work, getting ahead can be just so much "pie in the sky," or something wonderful that is out of reach. If you don't succeed, you may have to eat "humble pie," or face the consequences. Julia put all her dough in flour when she opened her own pastry shop. She kept her finger in the pie by baking every day, and eventually life became easy as pie, while her lazy competitor, Fanny, dreamed of pie in the sky and ended up eating a slice of humble pie.

Rather than a sweet pumpkin pie with a flaky crust and whipped cream, colonial historians believe the Pilgrims boiled chunks of the vegetable for the harvest meal. The

dish may have resembled the following recipe, one of the few to come down to us from the New England Pilgrims. Why not pitch in with friends and family and recreate the spirit of the first harvest meal by offering this updated Pilgrim staple at your next Thanksgiving dinner?

New England Classic Pompions

8 cups peeled diced pumpkin
¼ cup water
2 tbsp. butter
2 tbsp. vinegar
⅓ cup brown sugar
¼ tsp. ground ginger
¼ tsp. cinnamon
salt to taste

Put 2 cups of the diced pumpkin and ¼ cup water in a pot and cook mixture slowly over low heat until the pumpkin is tender. Slowly add the remaining 6 cups of pumpkin and continue to cook about thirty minutes, or until the pumpkin is soft but not mushy. The pumpkin pieces should retain their original shape. Remove the pot from the heat and add the rest of the ingredients. Stir and serve.

Hear ye! Hear ye!
We'll end with a PARADE
at the FOOTBALL stadium!
Gather your ANCESTORS!

Parade

The word *parade* marched into English from the Latin word *parare* and the French *parade*. In early Latin *parare* meant "to get ready," or prepare. Later, its usage suggested "to deck or adorn." The French *parade* included several diverse meanings: a display, gathering troops for inspection, a public square, street, or area for shops, and teaching a horse to stop.

Nearly a century and a half ago, Alfred Lord Tennyson used the word in his poem *In Memoriam* in the sense of displaying or showing off: "Let him be,/He loves to make parade of pain."

When we think of *parade*, it's of bright balloons, floats, resounding drums, marching bands, and strutting majorettes.

The distinction of the oldest Thanksgiving Day parade goes to the one held by Gimbel's department store in Philadelphia in 1920. The first Macy's parade in New York City, in 1924, drew ten thousand people. Today over 2 million people line up to view the parade and another 80 million watch it on television.

Football

For some sports-minded Americans, a close second to turkey as a favorite Thanksgiving tradition would be the afternoon football game. People have been kicking a ball, from Middle English *bal* and Old English *bealluc*, "testis," with their foot—Old English *fot*—for centuries

The Pilgrims would have been exposed to games played with the feet in England, yet there is no indication they scored any touchdowns during the harvest celebration. Although the Pilgrims worked hard, they did allow some rec reation, primarily ones that involved "wit and industry."

Today no Thanksgiving is complete without television networks vying for their share of the football audience. However, before football became instilled as the national Thanksgiving sport, local baseball teams provided the holiday festivities.

During the 1880s, the baseball diamond finally lost out to the gridiron as the official Thanksgiving sport, when college football teams initiated an annual game.

Ancestor

The word *ancestor* put down its roots from Latin *antecessor*—*ante*, "before," and *cedere*, "to go." The study of a family's ancestral history is called *genealogy*, from two Greek words: *genea*, "race," and *logy*, "word." The science of genealogy is a little like putting together the pieces of an elaborate puzzle.

Were you ever curious about your grandparents? Where and how they lived as youngsters and who their parents were? Presidents Taylor, Grant, Taft, and F. D. Roosevelt all claimed descendency from *Mayflower* passengers. Did you ever wonder if any of *your* ancestors were related to any of the passengers? If so, you might consider digging into your roots and putting together an ancestral family tree.

In the process of peeling away the layers of history, you'll not only learn about your particular family, but you'll get a fascinating look at the culture and history that shaped their lives. And compiling a family tree will enable you to pass along this special legacy to your descendants.

Finding out about your ancestors is something you can tackle inexpensively, either on your own or working with family members or classmates. The most important ingredient is perseverance.

The bare bones of any genealogical search are birth, marriage, and death certificates. All states are required to keep these vital statistics, so try to get this information first. In smaller cities, the county clerk's office is the source for birth and death records, which are usually available beginning in 1900. In larger cities, vital statistics are kept by the city health or vital statistics office. To find out where to write for these records, check your library for *The Vital Record Compendium*, by John D. and E. Diane Stemmons, or write for a booklet from the United States Department of Health and Human Services titled "Where to Write for Vital Records: Births, Deaths, Marriages, and Divorces," available for $3.25 from the Superintendent of Documents, U.S. Government Printing Office, Washington, D.C. 20402. If you find specific information that indicates your roots are linked to one of the Pilgrim families (see pages 32–33 for family names), contact The General Society of Mayflower Descendants, P.O. Box 3297, Plymouth, MA 02361, for more information.

Timeline

This chart is meant to give readers a general time frame as well as specific points of reference to topics mentioned in this book.

4000 B.C.	Sumerians settle Babylon
2500–2001	Earliest Egyptian mummies
c.800	Celts move into England
c.500	Ball games are played in Greece
0	The traditional beginning of the Christian era
A.D. 450	Old English begins to develop in the British Isles
550	Chess is first played in India
748	First newspaper is printed in Peking, China
851	Crossbow used in France
1000	Potatoes and corn planted in Peru
1517	Protestant Reformation begins in Germany when Martin Luther posts theses in Wittenberg
1520	Pope Leo X excommunicates Martin Luther
1524	Turkeys from South America eaten for the first time at Henry VIII's English court
1528	Protestant Reformation begins in Scotland
1533	Henry VIII secretly marries Anne Boleyn
1543	First Protestants burned at the stake during period of Spanish Inquisition

1557	Europe is hit with widespread influenza epidemic
1560–1660	Beginnings of Puritanism in England
1565	Sweet potatoes introduced into England
1589	Forks used for first time in French court
1605	French explorer Samuel de Champlain explores site of future Plymouth Harbor
1607	Religious separatists, hounded by James I, leave English Midlands
1620	Pilgrims sail from Plymouth, England, for America French nobles revolt against Louis XIII Oliver Cromwell denounced in England for playing cricket Famous artists working include the Italian sculptor Gian Bernini and Flemish painters Peter Paul Rubens and Sir Anthony Van Dyck
May 6, 1621	*Mayflower* returns to London
Fall 1621	Pilgrims hold three-day harvest festival
July 30, 1623	Pilgrims observe the first official Thanksgiving
1624	First cattle reach Plymouth
1636	Puritan Roger Williams banished from Massachusetts
1650	Population of world: 500 million
1651	Publishers and printers start book trade
1658	Oliver Cromwell dissolves English Parliament
1666	Great fire of London

1686	King James II establishes Federation of New England to remodel colonies in North America
1691	Plymouth Colony joins Massachusetts Bay Colony
1712	Last victim executed for witchcraft in England
1779	First sweet corn brought to New England
1780	Forks become a luxury symbol in France
1783	Great Britain recognizes United States independence
1793	Marie Antoinette and Louis XVI executed in France
1828	Noah Webster's *American Dictionary of the English Language* is published
1835	Hans Christian Andersen's tales for children appear
1841	First women receive university degrees in U.S.
1846	Iowa, the corn state, officially becomes a U.S. state
1850	Population of world: 1.1 billion; 3.2 million black slaves in U.S.
1869	Princeton and Rutgers originate intercollegiate football at New Brunswick, New Jersey
1872	First international soccer game, England vs. Scotland
1880	Canned meats and fruits appear in grocery stores
1895	First professional football game played in Latrobe, Pennsylvania
1914	Cape Cod Canal opens between Cape Cod and Buzzard's Bay

1916	First Rose Bowl football game played
1920	First Thanksgiving parade, in Philadelphia
1921	KDKA in Pittsburgh broadcasts first radio program
1924	Macy's first annual Thanksgiving Day parade
1928	First scheduled television broadcast in Schenectady, NY
1950	Population of world: 2.4 billion
1968	Spacecraft *Surveyor* 7 lands on the moon
1978	World Population: 4.4 billion (200,000 people added each day)
1986	Heaviest dressed turkey, eighty-one pounds, one quarter ounce, in Cheshire, England
1991	Population of world: _____ based on above figures You figure it out!

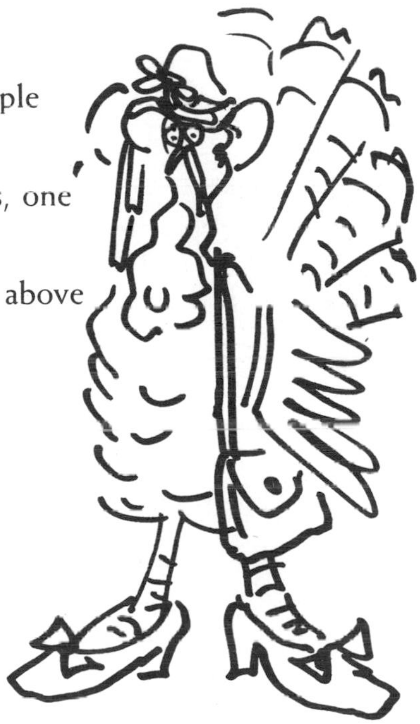

Bibliography

ETYMOLOGY

Funk, Charles Earle, and Charles Earle, Jr. *Horsefeathers & Other Curious Words*. New York: Harper & Row, 1958.
Discusses the origins of some of our most familiar and curious phrases and terms.

The Oxford Dictionary of English Etymology. Oxford: Clarendon Press, 1966.
The shorthand version of the definitive twenty-volume set.

The Oxford English Dictionary. Second edition. Oxford: Clarendon Press, 1989.
No superlatives go far enough in describing the value of this authoritative dictionary, with its chronological listings of word uses.

THANKSGIVING INFORMATION AND LORE

Bradford, William. *Of Plymouth Plantation 1620–1647*. New York: The Modern Library, 1981.
   A remarkable work by a remarkable Pilgrim leader—and surprisingly readable in this well-annotated version.
Caffrey, Kate. *The Mayflower*. New York: Stein and Day, 1974.
   Exhaustively researched and informative.
Carpenter, Edmund Janes. *The Mayflower Pilgrims*. New York: The Abingdon Press, 1918.
   An old volume with a wealth of biographical facts.
Marble, Annie. *The Women Who Came in the Mayflower*. Boston: The Pilgrim Press, 1920.
   Insightful and fascinating.
Mourt's Relation. Cambridge, MA: Applewood Books, 1963.
   This first published account of the coming of the Pilgrims to the New World throws an invaluable floodlight on Pilgrim history.
The Oxford Dictionary of Quotations. Oxford: Oxford University Press, 1979.
   A valuable research tool that organizes quotes alphabetically by author, comprehensively indexed.
Panati, Charles. *Extraordinary Origins of Everyday Things*. New York: Harper & Row, 1987.
   A fascinating and readable account of how hundred of commonplace items came into being.
Young, Alexander, ed. *Chronicles of the Pilgrim Fathers*. Reprint. Baltimore: Genealogical Publishing Company, 1974.
   A well-researched, accurate compilation of documents that relate to the Plymouth settlement.

Suggestions for Additional Reading

Appelbaum, Diana Karter. *Thanksgiving: An American History*. New York: Facts on File Publications, 1984.

Barth, Edna. *Turkeys, Pilgrims, and Indian Corn: The Story of the Thanksgiving Symbols*. New York: Seabury Press, 1975.

Crandall, Dr. Ralph. *Shaking Your Family Tree*. Camden, Maine: Yankee Books, 1986.

Fleming, Thomas J. *One Small Candle*. New York: W. W. Norton & Company, Inc., 1963.

Gill, Crispin. *Mayflower Remembered*. New York: Taplinger Publishing Company, 1970.

Harris, John. *Saga of the Pilgrims*. Chester, CT: Globe Pequot Press, 1990.

Rutman, Darrett B. *Husbandmen of Plymouth*. Boston: Beacon Press, 1967.

To help narrow the search for your roots, consult these books and publications:

Beller, Susan Provost. *Roots for Kids*. Betterway Publications, Inc., P.O. Box 219, Crozet, VA 22932.

Or check your public and school library for this very concise and helpful book.

Crandall, Dr. Ralph. *Shaking your Family Tree*. Camden, Maine. Yankee Books, 1986.

A terrific book for the beginner, illustrated with examples of discoveries.

Genealogical Books in Print, 6818 Lois Drive, Springfield, VA 22150.

Publishes a comprehensive listing of related books.

National Genealogical Society, 4527 Seventeenth Street N., Arlington, VA 22207

The umbrella organization that can steer you to regional offices and sources

Sources for Genealogical Forms and Supplies, Everton Publishers, P.O. Box 368, Logan, UT 84321

A good source for charts and forms to help you collect the data you need.

Index